TOP **10**
PARIS

CONTENTS

PARIS

INTRODUCING

The Sacré-Cœur in Montmartre

WELCOME TO
PARIS

Elegant, enchanting, irresistible: that's Paris. Here, you can admire world-famous art, glimpse iconic sights on a stroll along the Seine and linger over an *apéro* at a cosy café – all in one day. Don't want to miss a thing? With Top 10 Paris, you'll enjoy the very best the city has to offer.

As the French king Francis I once said "Paris is not a city; it's a world". And there sure is a lot to tempt travellers, whether it's magnificent monuments like the Arc de Triomphe or a slew of exceptional art museums, such as the Louvre. Housed in a Renaissance-style palace, the latter is the most visited museum in the world and overflows with masterpieces, from the *Venus de Milo* to the *Mona Lisa*. But in Paris great art isn't confined to museums and galleries. It's also found in the city's stunning places of worship, such as Notre-Dame and Sainte-Chapelle, and in its many restaurants, where

Paris-style café culture

talented chefs serve up beautifully prepared dishes. And then there's the city itself, a true architectural triumph thanks to the work of Baron Haussmann. One of the best places to view it? The iconic Eiffel Tower. This lofty iron structure attracts millions of visitors every year, who come to climb to the top of its cloud-scraping summit or to simply watch it sparkle across the Seine come nightfall.

Paris's famous sights are beyond doubt. But don't forget about its more understated charms. These can be found by wandering through the city's many elegant parks and gardens, window-shopping in the likes of super-chic Le Marais or by delving into an intimate basement club to catch some live jazz. There's also a diverse patchwork of neighbourhoods to explore, each with their own unique history and atmosphere, whether it's the historic Île de la Cité, artsy area of Montmartre or student-filled Latin Quarter. And there's also plenty to discover beyond the city's outskirts, including Père Lachaise Cemetery (the world's most visited necropolis) and the gilded palace of Versailles, former home of French royalty.

So, where to start? With Top 10 Paris, of course. This pocket-sized guide gets to the heart of the city with simple lists of 10, expert local knowledge, and comprehensive maps, helping you turn an ordinary trip into an extraordinary one.

THE STORY OF
PARIS

Starting life as a fishing settlement, Paris has seen many changes over its 2,500-year history. It's been a Roman stronghold, the heart of an empire and a cultural hub, and has weathered many cycles of revolution and rebellion. Here's the story of how it came to be.

The Birth of Paris

The Celtic Parisii tribe settled on the banks of the Seine in the 3rd century BCE, establishing a fishing community. In 52 BCE, the Romans conquered them, setting up an outpost called Lutetia, but by the 4th century CE, they had begun to refer to the city as Civitas Parisiorum – a name that morphed into Paris. The Roman Empire fell in 476 CE, after which the Franks claimed Paris. In 508, the city rose in importance when Frankish King Clovis I named it his capital.

Changing Fortunes

Over the next 500 years, Frankish dynasties rose and fell. In 987 CE, Hugh Capet was elected as king of the Franks, establishing the Capetian dynasty. During this time, the city became increasingly prosperous, largely thanks to the silver trade, and arts and culture thrived, with both Notre-Dame and the Sorbonne established. Yet by the 14th century, the city's fortunes had changed due to the ravages of the Black Death, which killed tens of thousands of Parisians in 1348, and the Hundred Years' War (1337–1453) with England.

A Cultural Hub

Following the war, much of Paris lay in ruins, with the French monarchy abandoning the city in favour of the

The Frankish King Clovis I, who ruled over Paris in the 6th century CE

Depiction of a battle during the Hundred Years' War

Loire. But it wasn't for long: after François I ascended the throne, Paris once again became the seat of the monarchy in 1528, and blossomed into the largest city in western Europe. Despite severe religious wars, Paris became a cultural hub: the nobility constructed mansions in the Marais and the king ordered the building of an elegant palace inspired by the Italian Renaissance (today's Louvre). Later, in the 17th century, Louis XIV cemented Paris's place as a world capital with the construction of the spectacular château and gardens at Versailles.

The Revolution
Towards the end of the 18th century, tensions began to rise in Paris. Public dissent had been fuelled by famine, war and excessive spending by the monarchy at Versailles. The situation was exacerbated by the ideas of the Enlightenment, which challenged the divine right of kings. Things came to a head on 14 July 1789, when Parisians revolted, storming the Bastille and kickstarting the French Revolution, which would last for 10 years. It was a time of great upheaval, with Louis XVI and Marie-Antoinette both killed by guillotine in 1793, and a controversial new government attempting to gain order over a city and a country divided by different ideologies.

Moments in History

259 BCE
Parisii settle on the banks of the River Seine.

845 CE
Vikings attack Paris, sacking the city after a siege.

1431
English Henry VI is crowned king of France and rules Paris for five years.

1528
François I transfers the seat of the French monarchy back to Paris.

1682
Louis XIV moves the French court and government to Versailles.

1789
The Bastille prison is stormed, igniting the French Revolution.

1799
Napoleon Bonaparte, commander of France's army, takes power in a coup d'état.

1889
Gustave Eiffel unveils the Eiffel Tower, a soaring structure built as part of the Paris Exposition.

1944
Paris is liberated from Nazi control by the Allies, following four years of occupation.

1968
Student protests take place in Paris, eventually transforming into a general strike.

2019
Notre-Dame suffers a terrible fire, destroying its roof and spire; plans to rebuild the cathedral are quickly undertaken.

Age of Empires

Following the revolution, military leader Napoleon Bonaparte took control in 1799, establishing a French Empire across much of western Europe. The riches that came with it funded growth and construction in Paris, including the building of the Arc de Triomphe. By 1815, however, following French defeat at the Battle of Waterloo, Napoleon was ousted and the monarchy reinstated – for a short time, at least. In 1851, Louis-Napoleon, nephew of Bonaparte, organized a successful coup d'état to be crowned Emperor Napoleon III. Under his rule – and with the help of architect Baron Hausmann – Paris was transformed, with sweeping boulevards, charming public squares and elegant Haussmann buildings constructed, making the city one of the most beautiful in the world. By 1860, towns such as Montmartre and Belleville had been incorporated into Paris, establishing the present-day city limits.

A Bohemian Belle Époque

The early 1870s saw Paris once again in upheaval, following war with the Prussians and the advent of the brief yet bloody Paris Commune, where the city's citizens rose up against the government. Following these events, a new Third Republic was established, which flourished during the belle

The French and English fighting at the Battle of Waterloo in 1815

Illustration of Paris's Eiffel Tower in 1889

époque (beautiful age) of the late 19th and early 20th centuries. During this time Paris pushed boundaries: the soaring Eiffel Tower was unveiled in 1889, the Metro opened in 1900 and bohemian Montmartre became a hotbed of artistic expression. Following World War I, a large number of artists and writers flocked to Paris, seeking inspiration, and the city developed a reputation for free-thinking and creativity.

Postwar Paris

On 14 June 1940, Nazi forces took control of Paris. Following occupation and the end of World War II, the city was shaken and subdued, with many of its beautiful buildings destroyed and some of its citizens left homeless. It slowly recuperated, however: modern quartiers, such as La Défense, were constructed, and in 1958, the Fifth Republic was established by Charles de Gaulle, with power split between an elected president and prime minister. Despite these reforms, social and political unrest was present throughout the 1960s, with many, especially students, commenting on the Algerian War of Independence and calling for

gender equality. As the decades wore on, meanwhile, art and culture continued to thrive, with some of the city's most famous museums, such as the Musée d'Orsay and Centre Pompidou, opening their doors.

Paris Today

Thanks to its continued interest in art and culture, and its central role in European affairs, Paris today is a modern and multicultural city. Like so many other world cities, it has faced challenges, including the 2015 Charlie Hebdo and Bataclan terrorist attacks, but it refuses to be cowed. Its revolutionary spirit lives on, through the *gilets jaunes* protests that began in 2018 and the Black Lives Matter demonstrations of 2020.

A memorial to victims of the Charlie Hebdo attacks

TOP 10
EXPERIENCES

Planning the perfect trip to Paris? Whether you're visiting for the first time or making a return trip, there are some things you simply shouldn't miss out on. To make the most of your time – and to enjoy the very best the city of light has to offer – be sure to add these experiences to your list.

1 Gaze at iconic artworks
Paris is synonymous with art, thanks to the city's many masterpiece-filled museums. There's the world-famous Louvre (p22), of course, but don't miss the Impressionist works at the Musée d'Orsay (p26) and the eye-catching Cubist pieces at the Musée Picasso (p40).

2 Wander along the Seine
Spot some of the city's most iconic landmarks – including Notre-Dame (p30) and the Eiffel Tower (p34) – on a flâne (stroll) along the Seine. In summer, riverside peniches (barges) serve up chilled wine, while in the winter, hot chocolates are sold from cafés on the quais.

3 Admire religious architecture
Some of the most beautiful buildings here are places of worship. Stop by Notre-Dame (p30), a Gothic masterpiece complete with grinning gargoyles, or head over to Sainte-Chapelle (p44), whose immense stained-glass windows refract light in every direction.

4 Listen to live jazz
Paris has thrummed with jazz music since the 1910s – and still does today. Drop into diminutive Baiser Salé (p67), which welcomes some of the best French and international jazz musicians, or spend the evening at Caveau de la Huchette (p67), a basement club that's hosted jazz since the 1950s.

5 Dine in a brasserie

To dine like a Parisian, make for a brasserie. These traditional restaurants serve up delicious helpings of French cuisine, including the likes of indulgent *confit de canard (p68)* and hearty *bœuf bourguignon*, alongside glasses of world-class French wine.

6 Shop in a Grand Magasin

Soak up some Parisian style by whiling away an hour or two in one of the city's famous Grand Magasins. Le Bon Marché *(p73)*, founded in 1838, is the most stylish of them all, offering everything from designer clothes to luxury jewellery and beyond.

7 Enjoy a traditional *apéro*

Enjoying a pre-dinner aperitif is a daily ritual for Parisians – and with wine from across the country on offer, it's always a real treat. For a glass with a view, take to the rooftop of Hôtel Dame des Arts *(p67)* or get cosy in the cave-like Verjus Bar à Vins *(p71)*.

8 Discover Parisian parks

Paris's numerous green spaces offer pockets of peaceful pleasure. Wander the Palais du Luxembourg's gardens *(p51)*, home to 17th-century manicured lawns, or explore the rose gardens and orangeries of former royal hunting ground Bois de Boulogne *(p160)*.

9 Sample the best patisserie

Sweet tooths rejoice: patisserie and Paris go hand-in-hand, with daintily decorated eclairs and pastel-coloured macarons both local favourites. They're always delicious, too, whether you're grabbing them from neighbourhood bakeries or celebrity *pâtissiers*.

10 Take in the view

Paris is widely regarded as one of the world's most beautiful cities, and there's no better way to appreciate this than by getting up high. Several of the city's landmarks offer bird's-eye views over the elegant skyline, including the iconic Eiffel Tower *(p34)*.

ITINERARIES

Admiring the *Mona Lisa*, enjoying pastries at a neighbourhood café, visiting the Eiffel Tower: there's a lot to see and do in Paris. With places to eat and drink, these itineraries offer ways to spend 2 days and 4 days in the capital.

2 DAYS

Day 1

Morning
With a patio spilling out among the elegant arcades of the Palais-Royal (*p107*), **Cafe Kitsune** (*maisonkitsune. com*) offers aromatic cups of coffee, alongside tempting French-Japanese fusion pastries. Fuelled up, head to the **Louvre** (*p22*), a short walk away, to see some of the world's most famous artworks, including the enigmatic *Mona Lisa* by Leonardo da Vinci. Afterwards, muse on all you've seen while wandering the tree-lined boulevards of the **Jardin des Tuileries** (*p105*); it was Paris's first garden to be made accessible to the public, under Louis XIV.

DRINK
If you need a pick-me-up after the Louvre, head to Angelina's (*226 Rue de Rivoli*). A Parisian institution, it offers thicker-than-soup hot chocolate in teapots, served with lashings of Chantilly.

Afternoon
Minutes away is Rue Saint-Honoré, a pretty street where you can fill up on soufflé at **Le Soufflé** (*lesouffle.fr*). Walk off your lunch with a pleasant *flâne* (stroll) west along the Seine, lined by *bateaux-mouches* (pleasure boats) and *peniches* (barges). From the Pont de l'Alma, take a short bus ride to reach the **Arc de Triomphe** (*p38*), Napoleon's towering monument to his army. The ground level is free to visit or, for spectacular views, purchase a ticket to climb the 284 steps to the top of the arch. As the sun sets, head back to the Seine for an evening cruise onboard the all-electric **Ducasse sur Seine** (*p67*). Here, as you dine on haute cuisine, the boat glides silently past some of the city's most famous sights, including the **Eiffel Tower** (*p34*), which crackles with light every hour come nightfall.

Day 2

Morning
Grab breakfast at little **Cuppa Café Paris** (*86 Rue de l'Université*), then stroll to the nearby **Musée d'Orsay** (*p26*). As one of

Aerial view over the city's imposing Arc de Triomphe

Paris's most famous galleries, it's very popular, so remember to book a timed ticket in advance. Inside, two highlights are the sculpture-filled entrance hall and the Impressionist floor, with works by both Monet and Manet. Back outside, a leisurely walk of 25 minutes or so takes you to picture-perfect St Germain for lunch at **Le Comptoir du Relais** (*p141*), whose set lunch menu is good value.

Afternoon

Walk over to the **Panthéon** (*p42*). Modelled after the one in Rome, this impressive building is the final resting place of some of France's most famous writers, including Alexandre Dumas and Victor Hugo. From here, head on foot to Île de la Cité, where you can step inside **Sainte-Chapelle** (*p44*) to admire its stunning stained-glass windows. After, pass by the sculpted Gothic cathedral of **Notre-Dame** (*p30*) as you make for Place des Vosges (*p95*), the oldest public square in Paris. The streets splitting off this symmetrical square overflow with restaurants, including the excellent **l'Ambroisie** (*p103*) – save room for its delicious chocolate tart.

Taking in the grandeur of the Panthéon

> ### SHOP
> A short stroll from Sainte-Chapelle and Notre-Dame is the fragrant Marché aux Fleurs Reine Elizabeth II (*p81*). Housed in three wrought-iron pavilions, it's the perfect place to pick up a bouquet of beautiful blooms or a new plant.

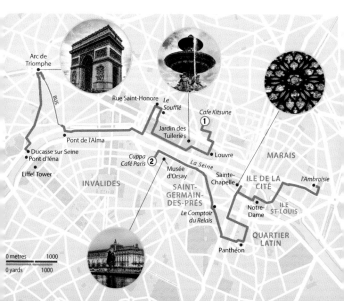

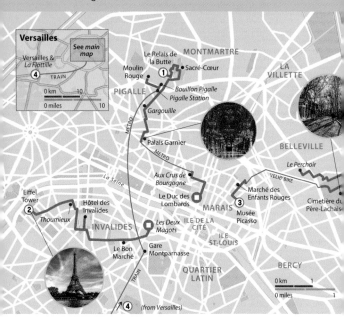

4 DAYS

Day 1

Amble along the cobbled streets of Montmartre, a charming neighbourhood sprinkled with independent cafés and artsy galleries. Grab a pavement table at **Le Relais de la Butte** (p157) to have coffee and babka, then visit the **Sacré-Cœur** (p36). This sublime basilica, made of white limestone, offers great views from its lofty dome. Next, stop in at cute **Gargouille** (p157) for a delicious lunch of Mediterranean sharing plates, then amble to the **Palais Garnier** (p106); this opulent opera house and theatre is best explored on a guided tour, which takes in the building's gilded auditorium and grand staircase. Afterwards, let the metro whisk you away to **Aux Crues de Bourgogne** (p93), a welcoming bistro offering traditional French favourites.

Still have some energy? Enjoy a jazz performance at intimate **Le Duc des Lombards** (ducdeslombards.com).

Day 2

Today begins with the iconic **Eiffel Tower** (p34). Each of its three floors offer spectacular vistas across the city, but for the best, make your way to the top floor, which sits at 276 m (906 ft).

Looking up towards the striking dome of the Sacré-Cœur

DRINK
After a nightcap? Make for Café de Flore (p139), found next door to Les Deux Magots. Set up in the 1880s, it was once a hub for writers and artists, and today serves up delicious cocktails.

Back on solid ground, head for the Art Deco-inspired **Thoumieux** (p131) for a traditional lunch. Refuelled, it's on to the **Hôtel des Invalides** (p46), a magnificent 17th-century building known for its eye-catching golden dome. It was originally constructed to house injured and elderly war veterans, but today is home to several museums, including the Army Museum. It's on to **Le Bon Marché** (p73) next, Paris's finest and first department store; it's worth going just to admire the extravagant window displays, often put together by notable artists and designers. End your day at **Les Deux Magots** (p139), a famed establishment that was once the haunt of Paris's most renowned writers.

Day 3

Start with a stroll around Le Marais, one of the city's prettiest neighbourhoods. The area is home to the **Musée Picasso** (p40), filled with over 5,000 works by the famous artist. Spend the rest of the morning here, then pop over to **Marché des Enfants Rouges** (p103), a covered market with plenty of options for lunch. Next, hire a Velib' bike (p171) and cycle to tree-filled **Cimetière du Père Lachaise** (p161). It's the resting place of some of the most famous people to have lived in Paris, including singer Édith Piaf. While away a couple of hours here, then take a five-minute walk to **Le Perchoir** (p165); this rooftop restaurant is the perfect place to watch the sun set over the city.

Day 4

Take an early train to **Versailles** (p159), France's most visited monument. Built by the Sun King, Louis XIV, and later

One of the rooms found in the lavish palace of Versailles

home to Louis XVI and Marie-Antoinette, this glittering palace is filled with lavish rooms, including the spectacular Hall of Mirrors. Once you've had your fill, grab some lunch at La Flottille (laflottille.fr), a charming spot overlooking Versailles' Grand Canal. In the afternoon, explore the extensive grounds, which includes a formal garden complete with stunning fountains and sculptures. Don't miss the 17th-century orangery, whose citrus collection includes trees that are over 200 years old. As the afternoon comes to an end, head back to Paris, grabbing an early dinner at traditional bistro **Bouillon Pigalle** (p157) in Montmartre. End your weekend with a cabaret show at the iconic **Moulin Rouge** (p152).

TRANSPORT
To reach Versailles, take the RER C train. It runs roughly every 5–20 minutes from multiple stops in the city centre, including the Eiffel Tower, Invalides and Notre-Dame.

TOP 10 HIGHLIGHTS

The Eiffel Tower

EXPLORE THE
HIGHLIGHTS

There are some sights in Paris you simply shouldn't miss, and it's these attractions that make the Top 10. Discover what makes each one a must-see on the following pages.

❶ Musée du Louvre

❷ Musée d'Orsay

❸ Notre-Dame

❹ Eiffel Tower

❺ Sacré-Coeur

❻ Arc de Triomphe

❼ Musée Picasso

❽ The Panthéon

❾ Sainte-Chapelle

❿ Hôtel des Invalides

MONTMARTRE

PIGALLE

BLVD DE ROCHECHOUART

LA VILLETTE

RUE LA FAYETTE

Gare de l'Est

Canal Saint Martin

BOULEVARD DE LA VILLETTE

USSMANN

BLVD DES ITALIENS

BLVD POISSONNIERE

RUE DU QUATRE SEPTEMBRE

MIE DE L'OPERA

RUE REAUMUR

BLVD DE STRASBOURG

Canal Saint Martin

RUE DU FAUBOURG DU TEMPLE

BELLEVILLE

AVENUE DE LA REPUBLIQUE

BLVD DU TEMPLE

RUE DE RIVOLI

QUAI DU LOUVRE
Pont des Arts
Pont Neuf
QUAI DES GRANDS AUGUSTINS

RUE DU RENARD

MARAIS

RUE DE RIVOLI

BOULEVARD BEAUMARCHAIS

BLVD RICHARD LENOIR

ÎLE DE LA CITÉ

ÎLE ST-LOUIS

BLVD SAINT GERMAIN

RUE SAINT JACQUES

QUARTIER LATIN

La Seine

Gare de Lyon

Jardin du Luxembourg

BLVD SAINT MICHEL

Jardin des Plantes

RUE MONGE

BLVD DU MONTPARNASSE

BLVD ARAGO

RUE DES GOBELINS

BLVD SAINT-MARCEL

0 metres 500
0 yards 500

MUSÉE DU LOUVRE

📍 L2 🏛 Musée du Louvre, 75001 🕐 9am–6pm Wed–Mon (to 9:45pm Fri)
📅 1 Jan, 1 May, 25 Dec 🌐 louvre.fr ↗

First opened to the public in 1793 after the Revolution, the Louvre contains one of the most important art collections in the world. The museum, housed inside an exquisite Renaissance-style palace, is home to some 35,000 priceless objects, covering everything from French paintings to Islamic art.

1 Venus de Milo
This iconic statue of Greek goddess Aphrodite – later known as Venus by the ancient Romans – is the highlight of the museum's Greek antiques. It dates from the end of the 2nd century BCE and was discovered on the Greek island of Milos in 1820.

2 Marly Horses
Coustou's rearing horses being restrained by horse-tamers were sculpted in 1745 for Louis XIV's Château de Marly. Replicas of these stand near the Place de la Concorde.

3 Mona Lisa
Arguably the most famous painting in the world, Leonardo da Vinci's portrait of a Florentine noblewoman with an enigmatic smile (p25) has been beautifully

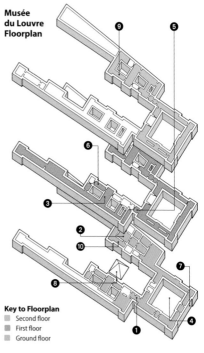

Musée du Louvre Floorplan

Key to Floorplan
- Second floor
- First floor
- Ground floor

restored. Visit early or late in the day.

4 Medieval Moats
An excavation in the 1980s uncovered the remains of the medieval fortress. You can see the base of the towers and the drawbridge support under the Cour Carrée.

5 The Winged Victory of Samothrace
This Hellenistic treasure, sculpted in the 3rd–2nd century BCE, stands atop a large stone ship radiating grace and power. It was created to commemorate a naval triumph at Rhodes.

> **TOP TIP**
>
> There's free access to the museum on Bastille Day (14 July).

Antique sculptures at the Musée du Louvre

GALLERY GUIDE
The main entrance is via the pyramid. There is also a less busy entrance at the Carrousel du Louvre (99 Rue de Rivoli). The Sully, Denon and Richelieu wings lead off from the foyer. The Petite Galerie, in the Richelieu wing, is an exhibition area aimed at children.

6 The Raft of the Medusa

The shipwreck of a French frigate three years earlier inspired this gigantic early Romantic painting by Théodore Géricault (1791–1824). Painted in 1819, the work depicts the moment when the survivors of the shipwreck spot a sail on the horizon.

7 Perrault's Colonnade

The majestic east façade by Claude Perrault (1613–88), with its four massive paired Corinthian columns, was originally part of an extension plan commissioned by Louis XIV.

8 Glass Pyramid

The unmistakable glass and steel pyramid, designed by I M Pei, became the Louvre's new entrance in 1989. Stainless steel tubes make up the 21-m- (69-ft-) high frame.

9 The Lacemaker

Jan Vermeer's masterpiece, painted around 1665, is a simple but beautiful rendering of everyday life in the Netherlands and is the highlight of the Louvre's Dutch painting collection.

10 Slaves

Michelangelo sculpted *Dying Slave* and *Rebellious Slave* (1513–20) for the tomb of Pope Julius II in Rome. The unfinished figures seem to be emerging from their "prisons" of stone.

Vermeer's *The Lacemaker* and (right) the *Dying Slave* by Michelangelo

Louvre Collections

1. French Paintings
This superb collection ranges from the 14th century to 1848 and includes works by such artists as Jean Watteau, Georges de la Tour and J H Fragonard.

2. French Sculpture
Highlights include the *Tomb of Philippe Pot* by Antoine le Moiturier, the *Marly Horses (p22)* and works by Pierre Puget.

3. Greek Antiquities
The art of Ancient Greece here ranges from a Cycladic idol from the 3rd millennium BCE to Classical Greek marble statues (c. 5th century BCE) and Hellenistic works (late 3rd–2nd century BCE).

4. Near Eastern Antiquities
This stunning collection includes a recreated temple of an Assyrian king and the Codex of Hammurabi (18th century BCE), humankind's oldest surviving written laws.

***Suger's Eagle*, an ancient Egyptian vase in the Egyptian antiquities collection**

5. Egyptian Antiquities
The finest collection outside Cairo, featuring a Sphinx in the crypt, the Seated Scribe of Sakkara, huge sarcophagi, mummified animals, funerary objects and intricate carvings depicting life in Ancient Egypt.

6. Italian Paintings
French royalty adored the art of Italy and amassed much of this collection (1200–1800). It includes many works by Leonardo da Vinci.

7. Italian Sculpture
Highlights of this collection, dating from the early Renaissance, include a 15th-century *Madonna and Child* by Donatello and Michelangelo's *Slaves (p23)*.

8. Dutch Paintings
Rembrandt's works are hung alongside domestic scenes by Vermeer and portraits by Frans Hals.

9. Objets d'Art
The ceramics, jewellery and other items in this collection encompass swathes of history.

10. Islamic Art
This exquisite collection, which spans 13 centuries and three continents, is covered by an ultra-modern glass veil.

Louvre Floorplan

Key to Floorplan
- Second floor
- First floor
- Ground floor
- Basement

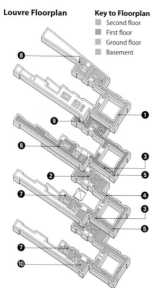

Famous Italian polymath Leonardo da Vinci, best known for his enigmatic painting, the *Mona Lisa*

LEONARDO DA VINCI AND THE MONA LISA

Born in Vinci to a wealthy family, Leonardo da Vinci (1452–1519) took up an apprenticeship under Florentine artist Andrea del Verrocchio, then served the Duke of Milan as an architect and military engineer, during which time he painted the *Last Supper* mural (1495). On his return to Florence, to work as architect to Cesare Borgia, he painted his most celebrated portrait, the *Mona Lisa* (1503–06). It is also known as *La Gioconda*, allegedly the name of the model's aristocratic husband, although there is ongoing speculation regarding the identity of the subject. The work, in particular the sitter's mysterious smile, shows mastery of two techniques: *chiaroscuro*, the contrast of light and shadow, and *sfumato*, subtle transitions between colours. It was the artist's own favourite painting and he took it with him everywhere. In 1516 François I brought both da Vinci and his beloved painting to France, giving him the use of a manor house in Amboise in the Loire Valley, where he died three years later.

TOP 10
WORKS BY DA VINCI
IN THE LOUVRE

1. *Mona Lisa* (1503–19)

2. *Saint John the Baptist* (1516)

3. *La Belle Ferronnière* (1490–97)

4. *Saint Anne* (1503–19)

5. *Virgin of the Spindle* (1510–30)

6. *The Virgin of the Rocks* (1483–85)

7. *Portrait of Isabelle d'Este* (1499–1500)

8. *The Virgin, the Child Jesus and Saint John the Baptist* (1520–40)

9. *Portrait of a Woman* (1500–1510)

10. *Bacchus* (1517–20)

The *Mona Lisa*, one of the Louvre's first paintings

MUSÉE D'ORSAY

📍 J2 🏠 Esplanade Valéry Giscard d'Estaing, 75007 🕐 9:30am–6pm Tue–Sun (to 9:45pm Thu) 🚫 1 May & 25 Dec 🌐 musee-orsay.fr 🔗

Housed in an elegant converted railway station overlooking the Seine, the Musée d'Orsay contains a world-class collection that covers a variety of art forms from 1848 to 1914. The museum's highlight is its wealth of Impressionist art, including iconic pieces by the likes of Monet, Degas and Van Gogh.

1 Le Déjeuner sur l'Herbe

French artist Edouard Manet's (1832–83) controversial painting (1863) was first shown in an "Exhibition of Rejected Works". Its bold portrayal of a classically nude woman enjoying the company of 19th-century men in suits brought about a wave of criticism.

> **GALLERY GUIDE**
> The upper level is home to the Impressionist and Post-Impressionist galleries, while the ground floor has Academic, Realist and Symbolist works. The ground floor has a boohshop and a giftshop.

2 A Burial at Ornans

This canvas depicting a sombre provincial funeral was painted by Gustave Courbet (1819-77) in 1849. Scorned by the establishment of the day, it is now seen as a landmark in French Realist painting.

3 The Building

The former railway station that houses this museum is almost as stunning as the exhibits. The light and spacious feel on stepping inside, after admiring the magnificent old façade, takes your breath away.

4 Blue Waterlilies

Claude Monet (1840–1926) painted this stunning canvas (1919) on one of his favourite themes. His love of waterlilies led him to create his own garden at Giverny in order to paint

Marble and bronze busts at the museum

them in a natural setting. This work inspired many abstract painters later in the 20th century.

5 Dancing at the Moulin de la Galette

One of the best-known paintings of the Impressionist era (1876), this work was shown at the Impressionist exhibition in 1877. The exuberance of Renoir's (1841–1919) work captures the mood of Montmartre and is considered one of the artist's masterpieces.

6 Degas' Statues of Dancers

The museum has an exceptional collection

Van Gogh's *Bedroom at Arles*

of works by Edgar Degas (1834–1917). Focusing on dancers and the world of opera, his sculptures range from innocent to erotic. *Young Dancer of Fourteen* (1881) was the only one exhibited during the artist's lifetime.

7 Jane Avril Dancing

Toulouse-Lautrec's (1864–1901) paintings define Paris's belle époque. Jane Avril was a famous Moulin Rouge dancer and featured in several of his works, like this 1895 canvas, which Toulouse-Lautrec drew from life, in situ at the cabaret.

8 La Belle Angèle

This stunning portrait of a Brittany beauty (1889) by Paul Gauguin (1848–1903) shows the remarkable influence Japanese art had on the artist's work. It was bought by Degas, to finance Gauguin's first trip to Polynesia.

9 Van Gogh Paintings

The star of the collection is Vincent van Gogh (1853–90) and the most striking of the canvases on display is the 1889 work showing the artist's *Bedroom at Arles*. Also on display are some of the artist's famous self-portraits, painted with his familiar intensity.

10 Café Campana

Offering a break from all the impressive art, the museum's café, renovated by the famous Campana Brothers, is delightfully situated behind one of the former station's huge clocks. A visit here is an experience in itself and the food is good too.

> **VIEW**
> The giant clock face inside the Café Campana offers fine views across Paris and its landmarks, including the Louvre and the Sacré-Coeur.

Young Dancer of Fourteen

Musée d'Orsay Collections

1. School of Pont-Aven
Paul Gauguin was at the centre of the group of artists associated with Pont-Aven in Brittany. His work here includes *Yellow Haystacks*, painted when the artist visited the region in 1889.

2. Art Nouveau
Art Nouveau is synonymous with Paris, with many metro stations retaining entrances built in the same style. Pendants by René Lalique (1860–1945) are among the examples on display here.

3. Symbolism
This vast collection includes works by artists such as Gustav Klimt (1862–1918) and Edvard Munch (1863–1944), as well as James Whistler's (1834–1903) portrait of his mother, dating from 1871.

4. Romanticism
The Romantics wanted to raise awareness about the spiritual world. One fine example is *The Tiger Hunt* (1854) by Eugène Delacroix (1798–1863).

5. The Impressionists
One of the best Impressionist collections in the world. Admirers of Manet, Monet and Renoir will not be disappointed.

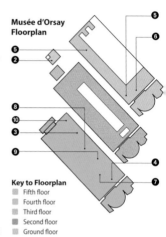

Musée d'Orsay Floorplan

Key to Floorplan
- Fifth floor
- Fourth floor
- Third floor
- Second floor
- Ground floor

6. The Post-Impressionists
The artists who moved on to a newer interpretation of Impressionism are equally well represented, including Matisse, Toulouse-Lautrec and the towering figure of Van Gogh.

7. Sculpture
The collection includes some beautiful pieces by Rodin and fantastic satirical carvings of politicians by Honoré Daumier (1808–79).

8. Naturalism
Naturalist painters intensified nature in their work. *Haymaking* (1877) by Jules Bastien-Lepage (1848–84) is a fine example.

9. Nabis
The Nabis Movement made art into a more decorative form. Pierre Bonnard (1867–1947) was one of its founding members.

10. Architecture
In addition to the 19th-century architectural etchings and drawings, there is a room dedicated to the creation of the Palais Garnier (106).

Blue Dancers (1890) by Degas, part of the museum's Impressionist collection

THE IMPRESSIONIST MOVEMENT

Regarded as the starting point of modern art, the Impressionist Movement is one of the best-known and best-loved art movements in the world – certainly if the popularity of the Musée d'Orsay is anything to go by. The movement emerged and developed in France during the late 19th and early 20th centuries, and almost all its leading figures were French. Some of the early artists of the movement included names such as Claude Monet, Pierre Auguste Renoir and Camille Pissarro. Impressionism was a reaction against the rigid formality and Classicism insisted upon by the Académie des Beaux-Arts in Paris, which was very much the art establishment, deciding what would or would not be exhibited at the Paris Salon. The term "Impressionism" was coined by a critic of the style, who dismissed the 1872 Monet painting *Impression: Sunrise*, now on display at the Musée Marmottan Monet (*p161*). The artists themselves then adopted the term. The style influenced Van Gogh and was to have a lasting influence on 19th- and 20th-century art.

Edouard Manet's famous Impressionist painting, *On the Beach* (1873)

NOTRE-DAME

📍 N4 🏠 6 Parvis Notre-Dame – Pl Jean-Paul II, 75004 🕐 Until late Dec 2024; chech website for details 🌐 notredamedeparis.fr ☑

The "heart" of the country, both geographically and spiritually, the Cathedral of Notre-Dame (Our Lady) sits majestically on the Île de la Cité. Famed for its stained glass, rose windows and grimacing gargoyles, it is a Gothic masterpiece – and one of Paris's most beloved sights.

1 Portal of the Last Judgment

This central relief over the doors of Notre-Dame depicts the biblical Last Judgment – when the souls of humankind will stand before God. The good souls move to the right, towards paradise, while the souls of the condemned move to the left and are led to hell. Though completely damaged during the Revolution, the portal was restored brilliantly in the 19th century.

2 The Towers

The Gothic towers are 69 m (226 ft) high; 387 steps within the north tower lead to great views. The south tower houses the Emmanuel Bell, forged in 1685 and rung on special occasions.

3 Gallery of Kings

The west façade of Notre-Dame cathedral is adorned with statues of the kings from the book of Judah. During the French Revolution the heads of these statues were chopped off, symbolically believed to be the kings of France. The missing heads were found nearly 200 years later at a construction site nearby and are now on display.

> **TOP TIP**
>
> Arrive early to visit the towers; the queue gets busy later in the day.

4 Flying Buttresses

The Gothic flying buttresses supporting the cathedral's east façade are by architect Jean Ravy. The best view is from Square Jean XXIII.

5 West Front

The entrance to the cathedral is through three elaborately carved

The cathedral's *chimères* watching over the city

portals. Biblical scenes, sculpted in the Middle Ages, depict the *Last Judgment*, the *Life of St Anne* and the *Life of the Virgin*.

6 Point Zero
Roads in France are measured from this plaque in front of the church, making it the very centre of the whole country – technically. Legend has it that any visitor who steps on it will inevitably return to Paris one day.

7 Portal of the Virgin
The splendid stone tympanum was carved in the 13th century and shows the Virgin Mary's death and coronation in heaven. However, the statue of the Virgin and Child that stands between the doors is a modern replica.

8 Rose Windows
Three great rose windows adorn the north, south and west façades, but only the north window retains its original 13th-century stained glass, depicting the Virgin surrounded by figures from the Old Testament. The south window shows Christ encircled by the Apostles.

9 Gargoyles
One of the key features of Gothic architecture, these grotesque statues stretch from the cathedral's roof and act as water spouts, channelling water off the roof. On a rainy day, visitors can see the water pouring from their mouths.

10 Galerie des Chimères
Lurking behind the upper gallery between the towers are large decorative sculptures or *chimères*. These were believed to ward off evil and were placed here to protect the cathedral.

> **EAT**
> A short walk from Notre-Dame is Le Petit Plateau (p85), where you can refuel with a tasty lunch. It also serves excellent cakes.

Clockwise from top right
Fantastic carvings on the Portal of the Virgin; the only remaining 13th-century rose window; the imposing West Front with its carved portals

Famous Visitors to Notre-Dame

1. François II and Mary Stuart
Mary Stuart (Mary Queen of Scots; 1542–87) had been raised in France and married the Dauphin in 1558. He ascended the throne as François II in 1559 and the king and queen were crowned in Notre-Dame.

2. Napoleon
The coronation of Napoleon (1769–1821) in Notre-Dame in 1804 saw the eager general seize the crown from Pope Pius VII and crown himself emperor and his wife, Josephine, empress.

3. Josephine
Josephine's (1763–1814) reign as Empress of France lasted only five years; Napoleon divorced her in 1809.

4. Pope Pius VII
In 1809 Pope Pius VII (1742–1823), who oversaw Napoleon's Notre-Dame coronation, was taken captive when the emperor declared the Papal States to be part of France. The pope was imprisoned at Fontainebleau.

5. Joan of Arc
The patriot Jeanne d'Arc (1412–31), who defended France against the invading English, had a posthumous trial here in 1455, despite having been burned at the stake 24 years earlier. She was found to be innocent of heresy.

6. Philip the Fair
In 1302 the first States General parliament was formally opened at Notre-Dame by Philip IV (1268–1314), otherwise known as Philip the Fair. He greatly increased the governing power of the French royalty.

General Charles de Gaulle visiting Notre-Dame cathedral in 1944

7. Charles de Gaulle
On 26 August 1944, Charles de Gaulle entered Paris and attended a Magnificat service to celebrate the liberation of Paris, despite the fact that hostile snipers were still at large outside the cathedral.

8. Henry VI of England
Henry VI (1421–71) became king of England at the age of one. Like his father, Henry V, he also claimed France and was crowned in Notre-Dame in 1430.

9. Marguerite of Valois
In August 1572, Marguerite (1553–1589), sister of Charles IX, stood in the Notre-Dame chancel during her marriage to the Protestant Henri of Navarre (1553–1610), while he stood alone by the door.

10. Henri of Navarre
As a Protestant Huguenot, Henri's marriage to the Catholic Marguerite resulted in uprising and many massacres. In 1589, he became Henri IV, the first Bourbon king of France, and converted to Catholicism, stating that "Paris is well worth a Mass".

Statue of Joan of Arc in the cathedral

SAVING NOTRE-DAME

Paris's great cathedral has had a history of deterioration and restoration. When Victor Hugo's classic *Notre-Dame de Paris (The Hunchback of Notre-Dame)* was first published in 1831, the cathedral was in a state of decay. Even for the crowning of Napoleon in 1804, the crumbling setting had to be disguised with ornamentation. Later, during the Revolution, the cathedral was sold to a scrap dealer, though fortunately not demolished. Hugo was intent on saving France's spiritual heart and helped mount a campaign to restore Notre-Dame before it was too late; Eugène Emmanuel Viollet-le-Duc (1814–79) was chosen to spearhead the restoration. Repairs began again in 2019 before the cathedral was damaged by fire. Within 24 hours of the blaze, President Macron vowed to rebuild Notre-Dame and more than €800 million was raised. At the same time, sales of Hugo's iconic novel rocketed, prompting French booksellers to ask for profits from renewed sales to be directed towards the restoration.

The 1956 screen adaptation of Hugo's *The Hunchback of Notre Dame*

EIFFEL TOWER

📍 B4 🏠 Champ de Mars, 7e 🕐 Hours vary, chech website
📅 14 Jul 🌐 toureiffel.paris 🔲🔲

A remarkable feat of engineering, the Eiffel Tower is the most distinctive symbol of Paris. The soaring structure, nick-named the "Iron Lady", stands 324 m (1,063 ft) high above Paris, offering unrivalled views over the city from each of its three levels.

1 Bust of Gustave Eiffel
This bust of the tower's creator, sculpted by Antoine Bourdelle, was placed below his achievement, by the north pillar, in 1929.

2 Gustave Eiffel's Office
Located at the top of the tower is Gustave Eiffel's office, which has been restored to its original condition. It displays wax models of Thomas Edison and Eiffel himself.

3 First Level
You can walk the 345 steps up to the 57-m- (187-ft-) high first level and enjoy a hearty meal at the all-day brasserie, which offers a menu focusing on local produce. This level also includes glass floors and educational displays.

4 Lighting
Some 20,000 bulbs and 336 lamps make the Eiffel Tower a spectacular night-time sight. It sparkles like a giant Christmas tree for five minutes every hour from dusk until 1am.

5 View from the Trocadéro
Day or night, the best approach for a first-time view of the tower is from the Trocadéro (p123), which affords a monumental vista from the Chaillot terrace across the Seine.

6 Second Level
At 116 m (380 ft) high, this level is the

Eiffel Tower, seen from
the Jardins du Trocadéro

> **DRINK**
> Level 3 has
> a champagne bar,
> where you can sip
> on a glass of bubbly
> while taking in
> spectacular views
> across the city.

location of Le Jules
Verne restaurant, one
of the finest in Paris
for food and views
(p131). It is reached by
a private lift in the
south pillar.

7 Champ de Mars

The long gardens
of this former parade
ground stretch from
the base of the tower
to the École Militaire
(military school).

8 Ironwork

The complex
pattern of the girders,
held together by 2.5
million rivets, stabilizes
the tower in high winds.
The metal can expand
up to 15 cm (6 in) on
hot days.

9 Hydraulic Lift Mechanism

The 1899 lift mechanism
is still in operation and
travels some 103,000 km
(64,000 miles) a year.
The uniformed guard
clinging to the outside
is a model.

10 Viewing Gallery

At 276 m (906 ft),
the stupendous view
stretches for 80 km
(50 miles) on a clear
day. You can also see
Gustave Eiffel's sitting
room on this level.

Clockwise from right
Intricate iron details of
the tower; a reconstruc-
tion of Gustave Eiffel's
office; bust of Gustave
Eiffel at the base of the
tower; stunning city
views from the tower

SACRÉ-COEUR

📍 F1 🏠 35 Rue du Chevalier-de-la-Barre, 75018 🕐 Basilica: 6:30am–10:30pm daily (last adm: 10:15pm) 🌐 sacre-coeur-montmartre.com 🔗

One of the city's most photographed sights, the spectacular white basilica of Sacré-Coeur (Sacred Heart) watches over Paris from its highest point. Constructed over 46 years, the basilica was built as a memorial to the 58,000 French soldiers killed during the Franco-Prussian War (1870–71).

1 Square Louise Michel

Just below the lovely Sacré-Coeur is this pretty garden lined by trees and home to an elegant fountain. Its 222 steps are a popular way to reach the basilica.

2 Crypt Vaults

The arched vaults of the crypt house a chapel that contains the heart of Alexandre Legentil, one of the strongest advocates of Sacré-Coeur.

3 Stained-Glass Gallery

One level of the great dome is encircled by stained-glass windows.

The tranquil interiors of the basilica

This level affords a beautiful view over the whole interior.

4 Façade

Renowned French architect Paul Abadie (1812–1884) employed a splendid mix of domes, turrets and Classical features in his design of this elegant basilica. It was constructed using Château-Landon stone, which secretes calcite when wet and keeps the façade bleached white.

5 Statue of Christ

Considered to be the basilica's most important statue, this shows Christ giving a blessing. It is symbolically placed in a niche over the main entrance, just above the two bronze equestrian statues.

Vibrant stained-glass window in the basilica

> 🚌 **TRANSPORT**
> To avoid the steep climb up to the basilica, take the Funiculaire de Montmartre cable railway. It cuts the ascent down to just a couple of minutes and can be accessed with a standard metro ticket. Catch the funicular from the end of Rue Foyatier, by Square Willette.

6 The Dome

🕑 May–Sep: 9:30am–8pm daily (Oct–April: to 5pm daily)

The distinctive egg-shaped dome of the basilica is the second-highest viewpoint in Paris after the Eiffel Tower. Reached via a spiral staircase, vistas can stretch as far as 48 km (30 miles) on a clear day.

7 Bell Tower

The *campanile*, designed by Lucien Magne and added in 1904, is 80 m (262 ft) high. One of the heaviest bells in the world, the 19-ton La Savoyarde hangs in the belfry. Cast in Annecy in 1895, it was donated by the dioceses of Savoy.

8 Equestrian Statues

Two striking bronze statues of French saints stand on the portico above the main entrance, cast in 1927 by Hippolyte Lefèbvre. One statue is of Joan of Arc, while the other is of Louis IX, who was later canonized as Saint Louis.

9 Great Mosaic of Christ

A glittering Byzantine mosaic of Christ, created by Luc Olivier Merson between 1912 and 1922, decorates the vault over the chancel. It represents France's devotion to the Sacred Heart.

10 Bronze Doors

The doors of the portico entrance are beautifully decorated

The basilica, crowned by its elegant ovoid dome

with floral carvings and bronze relief sculptures depicting the *Last Supper* and other scenes from the life of Christ.

Panoramic view of the city from the basilica's dome

ARC DE TRIOMPHE

◉ B2 ⌂ Pl Charles-de-Gaulle, 75008 ◷ 10am–10:30pm (Jun–Sep: to 11pm); booking essential ⓦ paris-arc-de-triomphe.fr ◿

Found at the eastern end of the Champs-Élysées, the Arc de Triomphe was built by Napoleon as a tribute to his Grande Armée. The imposing arch is decorated with sculptures depicting various battles and is home to the eternal flame of the Tomb of the Unknown Soldier.

 EAT
Opposite the Arc de Triomphe is the starting point for Bustronome, a bus that offers fine-dining as it goes around Paris.

1 Viewing Platform

Take the lift or climb 284 steps to the top of the Arc de Triomphe to get a sublime view of Paris and a sense of the arch's dominant position in the centre of the Place Charles de Gaulle. To the east is the Champs-Élysées (p113) and to the west is the Grande Arche of La Défense (p159). There are 40 steps after the lift.

2 Frieze

A frieze running around the arch shows French troops departing for battle (east) and their victorious return (west).

3 Museum

Within the arch is a small but interesting museum which tells the history of its construction and gives details of various celebrations and funerals that the arch has seen over the years. The more recent ones are shown in a video.

4 Departure of the Volunteers in 1792

One of the most striking sculptures is on the front right base. It is a depiction of French citizens leaving to defend their nation against Austria and Prussia.

5 Thirty Shields

Immediately below the top of the arch runs a row of 30 carved shields, each

THE GREAT AXIS

The Arc de Triomphe is the central of three arches; together they create a grand vision of which even Napoleon would have been proud. He was responsible for the first two, placing the Arc de Triomphe directly in line with the Arc de Triomphe du Carrousel in front of the Louvre (p22), which also celebrates the victory at Austerlitz. In 1989, the trio was completed with the Grande Arche de La Défense. The 8-km- (5-mile-) long *Grand Axe* (Great Axis) runs from here to the Louvre's Pyramid.

The two avenues, as seen from the viewing platform

The monumental Arc de Triomphe in the heart of Place Charles de Gaulle

carrying the name of a Napoleonic victory.

6 Triumph of Napoleon

As you look at the arch from the splendid Champs-Elysées (p113), J P Cortot's high-relief on the left base shows the restored *Triumph of Napoleon*. It celebrates the Treaty of Vienna peace agreement signed in 1810, when Napoleon's empire was in its heyday.

7 Battle of Aboukir

Above the *Triumph of Napoleon* carving is this scene showing Napoleon's victory over the Turks in 1799. The same victory was commemorated on canvas in 1806 by the French painter Antoine Gros and is now on display at the Palace of Versailles (p159).

 VIEW
Traffic is banned along the Champs-Élysées on the first Sunday of every month, making for a great photo of the Arc de Triomphe.

8 Battle of Austerlitz

Another battle victory is shown on a frieze on the arch's north side. It depicts Napoleon's heavily outnumbered troops breaking the ice on Lake Satschan in Austria, a tactic that led to thousands of enemy soldiers being drowned.

9 General Marceau's Funeral

Marceau died in battle against the Austrian army in 1796, after a famous victory against them the previous year. His funeral is depicted in a frieze located above the *Departure of the Volunteers in 1792*.

10 Tomb of the Unknown Soldier

In the centre of the arch flickers the eternal flame on the Tomb of the Unknown Soldier, a victim of World War I buried on 11 November 1920. It is symbolically reignited every day at 6:30pm.

Torch at the Tomb of the Unknown Soldier

MUSÉE PICASSO

📍 R2 🏠 5 Rue de Thorigny, 75003 🕐 10:30am–6pm Tue–Fri, 9:30am–6pm weekends and Parisian school holidays 🚫 On Mondays, 1 Jan, 1 May and 1 Dec 🌐 museepicassoparis.fr 🔲 🔲

Housed in the Hôtel Salé, a 17th-century mansion, this compelling museum is home to the largest collection of works by Pablo Picasso in the world. Covering a huge variety of styles and media, it offers an unparalleled insight into both the artist's creative process and his life in general.

1 Cubism
Of Picasso's many art styles, Cubism – an avant-garde, abstract approach – is what he's best known for. He began experimenting with this style in 1907, creating one of his most iconic Cubist works during the Spanish Civil War: a series depicting *The Weeping Woman* and the pain caused by General Francisco Franco.

2 Sculptures
The collection of around 250 sculptures, which spans much of Picasso's career, is a great way to witness the evolution of his style. Perhaps the most famous is the striking *Tête de Femme* (Head of a Woman), made from wood and plaster in 1931.

> ✂️ **EAT**
> Why not enjoy a snach and a coffee at the museum's self-service rooftop café? The stunning terrace here offers views of the Hôtel Salé's regal exterior.

3 The Blue Period
A sense of despair characterized Picasso's work at the start of the 20th century, a phase known as his "Blue Period". His 1901 self-portrait encapsulates this despondency; a stark painting on a dull blue background, Picasso is depicted with hollow eyes staring out from a pale face.

4 Surrealism
Picasso's exploration of Surrealism started in 1924 and was influenced

Picasso's striking *Femmes à leur Toilette*

by other artists, notably Salvador Dalí; he continued to dabble with this style until his death. The 1925 painting *Le Baiser* (The Kiss) is one of his most famous Surrealist works.

5 Engravings
Picasso made engravings – such as lithographs and linocuts – throughout his career. In his final years, the number he produced accelerated, and from 1968 to 1972 he created hundreds of erotic engravings, many of which are on display here.

6 Personal items
Many postcards and letters are on display throughout the museum, providing an insight into Picasso's private life. In addition, some of the artist's original tools and paintbrushes are on display in the studio section of the museum.

7 Photography
Picasso took many of the photos displayed in the museum himself, including some of his own works, which helped him study and improve upon his creations. Other photographs include some of the artist himself by notable 20th-century photographers, such as Henri Cartier-Bresson.

8 Picasso's art collection
Alongside the artist's own works, the museum is also home to pieces from his extensive personal art collection. Among them are paintings by the likes of Miró, Renoir, Matisse and Cézanne, and drawings by artists such as Degas and Giacometti.

9 Temporary exhibitions
At least one temporary exhibition usually runs alongside the permanent collection. These are often linked to Picasso's work, such as pieces from

PICASSO IN FRANCE

Born in Malaga, Spain, Picasso move to Paris in 1904, before later settling in the south of France. After 1934, he never returned to his homeland due to his rejection of the regime of General Franco. However, throughout his life in France he used Spanish themes in his art, such as the bull and the guitar, which he associated with his Andalusian childhood. Upon his death in 1973, the French state inherited many of his works in lieu of death duties, which it used to establish the Musée Picasso in 1985.

other artists experimenting with one of the styles he was famous for, including Cubism, or additional touring pieces from the artist himself.

10 The building
Known as the Hôtel Salé, the stately mansion housing the museum was built in 1656 for Aubert de Fontenay, a salt-tax collector (*salé* means "salty"). Many original features have been preserved, including the sweeping staircase.

The stunning main staircase in the museum

THE PANTHÉON

📍 N6 🏠 Pl du Panthéon, 75005 🕐 10am–6:30pm daily (Oct–Mar: to 6pm)
📅 1 Jan, 1 May, 25 Dec 🌐 paris-pantheon.fr 📷📷

Originally built as a church, this magnificent building was intended to look like the Pantheon in Rome, but more closely resembles St Paul's Cathedral in London. Today a public building, it provides a fitting final resting place for the nation's great figures, including Voltaire, Victor Hugo and Émile Zola.

1 Crypt
The crypt is eerily impressive in its scale, compared to most tiny, dark church crypts. Here lie the tombs of and memorials to worthy French citizens, including the prolific writer Emile Zola.

2 Tomb of Voltaire
A marble statue of the great writer, wit and philosopher Voltaire (1694–1788) stands in front of his tomb.

The building's Neo-Classical façade

3 Façade
The Panthéon's façade was inspired by Roman architecture. The 22 Corinthian columns support both the portico roof and bas-reliefs.

Statue of Voltaire

4 Pediment Relief
The bas-relief above the entrance shows a female figure, representing France, handing out laurels to the patriots of the nation – as was the practice in ancient Greece and Rome.

TOP TIP

From April to October, visitors can visit the dome for an extra fee.

St Geneviève, the patron saint of Paris. She is believed to have saved the city from invasion by Attila the Hun and his hordes in 451 through the power of her prayers.

5 Frescoes of Sainte Geneviève
Murals by 19th-century French artist Pierre Puvis de Chavannes, on the nave, tell the story of

6 Dome
Inspired by Sir Christopher Wren's design for St Paul's

Foucault's pendulum hanging from the dome

The Panthéon Floorplan

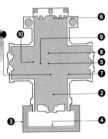

Cathedral in London, as well as by the Dôme Church at the Hôtel des Invalides (*p46*), this iron-framed dome is made up of three layers. At the top, a narrow opening lets in only a tiny amount of natural light, in keeping with the building's sombre purpose.

7 Dome Galleries

A staircase leads to the galleries located directly beneath the dome, and provides spectacular 360-degree views of Paris. The pillars surrounding the galleries are both decorative and functional, providing essential support for the dome.

8 Foucault's Pendulum

In 1851 French physicist Jean Foucault (1819–68) followed up an earlier experiment to prove the Earth's rotation by hanging his famous pendulum from the dome of the Panthéon. The plane of the pendulum's swing rotated 11 degrees clockwise each hour in relation to the floor, thereby proving Foucault's all-important theory.

9 Women's Tombs

Actor and dancer Josephine Baker was interred here in 2021. She was the first woman of colour to be buried in the Panthéon – and is one of only six women in total.

10 Tomb of Victor Hugo

The body of the French author was carried to the Panthéon in a pauper's hearse, at his own request.

LOUIS BRAILLE

One of the most influential citizens buried in the Panthéon is Louis Braille (1809–52). Braille became blind at the age of three. He attended the National Institute for the Young Blind and continued there as a teacher. In 1829, he had the idea of adapting a coding system in use by the army, by turning letters into raised dots. Reading Braille has transformed the lives of blind people ever since.

SAINTE-CHAPELLE

📍 N3 🏠 10 Blvd du Palais, 75001 🕐 Daily; hours vary, check website
🌐 sainte-chapelle.fr

Built by Louis IX in the 13th century, ethereal Sainte-Chapelle was once likened to "a gateway to heaven" by the city's devout. Today, this Gothic masterpiece is considered the most beautiful church in Paris, not least for its 15 stunning stained-glass windows and star-covered vaulted ceiling.

1 Upper Chapel Entrance
As you emerge, via a spiral staircase, into this airy space, the effect of light and colour is utterly breathtaking. The 13th-century stained-glass windows, the oldest surviving in Paris, separated by stone columns, depict biblical scenes from Genesis right through to the Crucifixion. To "read" the windows, start with the lower left panel and then follow each row left to right, from bottom to top.

2 Window of Christ's Passion
Located above the apse, this stained-glass depiction of the Crucifixion is the most beautiful window in the chapel.

3 Lower Chapel
Intended for use by the king's servants, and dedicated to the Virgin Mary, this chapel is not as light and lofty as the Upper Chapel but is still a magnificent sight.

4 Main Portal
Like the Upper Chapel, the main portal has two tiers. Its pinnacles are decorated with a crown of thorns as a symbol of the relics within.

5 The Spire
The pencil-thin shape and open lattice-work give the *flèche* (spire) a very delicate appearance. In fact, three earlier church spires burned down – this one was erected in 1853 and rises to 75 m (245 ft).

EAT
To experience a little 1920s-style elegance, visit Brasserie Les Deux Palais on the corner of the Boulevard du Palais and Rue de Lutèce.

The church's awe-inspiring stained-glass windows

6 St Louis' Oratory

In the late 14th century Louis XI added an oratory where he could attend Mass through a small grille in the wall. The chapel originally adjoined the Conciergerie (p81), the former royal palace on the Île de la Cité.

7 Rose Window

The Flamboyant rose window, depicting St John's vision of the Apocalypse in 86 superb panels, was a gift from Charles VIII in 1485. The green and yellow hues are brightest at sunset.

8 Evening Concerts

Sainte-Chapelle has excellent acoustics. Classical concerts are held regularly here from March until December.

9 Seats of the Royal Family

During Mass, the royal family sat in niches in the fourth bays on both sides of the chapel, away from the congregation.

10 Apostle Statues

Carved medieval statues of 12 apostles stand on the pillars along the walls. Badly damaged in the Revolution, most have been restored: the bearded apostle, fifth on the left, is the only original statue.

> **TOP TIP**
>
> Carry a pair of binoculars to view the church's uppermost glass panels.

> **RELICS OF THE PASSION**
>
> Louis IX, later St Louis, was the only French king to be canonized. While on his first Crusade in 1239, he purchased the alleged Crown of Thorns from the Emperor of Constantinople, and subsequently other relics, including pieces of the True Cross, nails from the Crucifixion and a few drops of Christ's blood, paying almost three times more for them than for the construction of Sainte-Chapelle itself. The relics resided in Notre-Dame and were rescued from the destructive fire in 2019.

Clockwise from bottom right **Sainte-Chapelle with the Palais de Justice in the foreground; carved statue of an apostle on a pillar; beautiful stained-glass rose window**

HÔTEL DES INVALIDES

📍 D4 🏠 129 Rue de Grenelle, 75007 or 6 Blvd des Invalides, 75007
🕐 10am–6pm daily (to 10pm on the first Fri of every month) 🚫 1 Jan,
1 May, 25 Dec 🌐 musee-armee.fr 🔗

Topped by a golden dome, this impressive complex was built in the late 17th century for wounded soldiers. Today, it attracts visitors with its many military museums, including the Musée de l'Armée, and the Dôme des Invalides, the final resting place of Napoleon Bonaparte.

1 Invalides Gardens

The approach to the Hôtel is across public gardens and then through a large gate into the Invalides Gardens themselves.

SHOP
The hotel giftshop sells books on the Musée de l'Armée's extensive collections, as well as postcards, figurines and posters.

Designed in 1704, their paths are lined by cannons dating from the 17th and 18th centuries.

2 Golden Dome

The second church at the Hôtel was begun in 1677 and took 27 years to build. Its magnificent dome is 107 m (351 ft) high. Wrapped in luxurious gold leaf, the dome glistens as much now as it did when Louis XIV, the Sun King, had it first gilded in 1715.

Napoleon's tomb made of red porphyry in the crypt

3 Napoleon's Tomb

Napoleon's body was brought here from St Helena in 1840, some 19 years after he died.

DRINK
Le Café du Musée, near Musée Rodin (p128), is a lovely spot known for its varied menu of delicious cocktails, wines and beers.

Charles de la Fosse's *Saint Louis in Glory*, Dôme Church

He rests in a cocoon of six coffins, almost "on the banks of the Seine", as was his last wish.

4 Musée de l'Armée

The Army Museum (p127) is one of the largest collections of militaria in the world. Enthusiasts will be absorbed for hours, and even the casual visitor will enjoy the exhibits. The Département Moderne, which traces military history from Louis XIV to Napoleon III, is also worth a visit.

5 Dôme Church Ceiling

The colourful, circular painting on the interior of the dome above the crypt is the intricate *Saint Louis in Glory* painted in 1692 by the renowned French artist Charles de la Fosse. Near the centre is St Louis, who represents Louis XIV, handing his sword to Christ in the presence of the Virgin Mary and angels.

6 Hôtel des Invalides

One of the loveliest sights in Paris, the Classical façade of the Hôtel is four floors high and almost 200 m (645 ft) wide end to end. Features include the dormer windows with their variously shaped shield surrounds.

7 Musée de l'Ordre de la Libération

The Order of Liberation, France's highest military honour, was created by Charles de Gaulle in 1940 to acknowledge contributions during World War II. The museum details the history of the honour and the wartime Free French movement.

The imposing Hôtel des Invalides

8 Church Tombs

Encircling the Dôme Church are the tombs of French soldiers, such as Marshal Foch and Marshal Vauban, who revolutionized military fortifications and siege tactics.

9 St-Louis-des-Invalides

Adjoining the Dôme Church is the Invalides complex's original church, worth seeing for its 17th-century organ, on which the first performance of Berlioz's *Requiem* was given.

10 Musée des Plans-Reliefs

Maps and models of French forts and fortified towns are displayed here. Some of them are beautifully detailed, such as the oldest model on display, of Perpignan, dating from 1686.

Hôtel des Invalides Floorplan

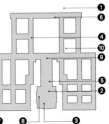

TOP 10 OF EVERYTHING

A coffee and a croissant

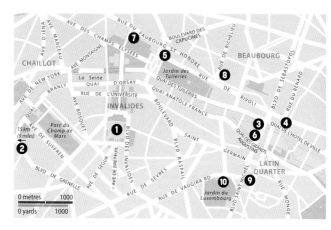

HISTORIC BUILDINGS

1 Hôtel des Invalides
This imposing building (p46) is topped with a golden dome that can be seen across the rooftops of Paris.

2 Versailles
Louis XIV turned his father's old hunting lodge into the largest palace (p159) in Europe and moved his court here in 1678. It was the royal residence for more than a century until Louis XVI and his queen Marie-Antoinette fled during the Revolution.

3 Conciergerie
Originally home to the keeper of the king's mansion and guards of the Palais de Justice, the Conciergerie (p81) became a prison at the end of the 14th century. More than 4,000 citizens (including Marie-Antoinette) were held prisoner here during the Revolution, half of whom were guillotined. It remained a prison until 1914.

4 Hôtel de Ville
📍 P3 🏠 4 Pl de l'Hôtel de Ville, 75001 🕐 For group tours and temporary exhibitions 🌐 paris.fr 📷
Paris's city hall sports an elaborate façade, with ornate stonework, statues and a turreted roof. It is a 19th-century reconstruction of the original town hall, which was burned down during the Paris Commune of 1871. Book ahead for guided tours. The square in front was once the site of executions: Ravaillac, assassin of Henri IV, was quartered alive here in 1610.

5 Hôtel de la Marine
📍 D3 🏠 2 Pl de la Concorde, 75008 🕐 10:30am–7pm daily (to 9:30pm Fri) 🌐 hotel-de-la-marine.paris
The Hôtel de la Marine is a colonnaded 18th-century building, which used to be

The striking Conciergerie, overlooking the Seine

the royal Garde Meuble (storehouse) and then the ministry of naval affairs. Its beautifully restored reception rooms and apartments are open to the public.

6 Palais de Justice

The building that now houses the French law courts and judiciary (p82) dates back to the Roman times. It was the royal palace until the 14th century, when Charles V moved the court to the Marais. During the Revolution, thousands were sentenced to death in the Première Chambre Civile, allegedly the former bedroom of Louis IX.

7 Palais de l'Élysée

This imposing palace (p115) has been the official residence of the president of the French Republic since 1873. It was built as a private mansion in 1718 and was owned by Madame de Pompadour, mistress of Louis XV, who extended the English-style gardens as far as the Champs-Élysées. After the Battle of Waterloo in 1815, Napoleon signed his second and final abdication here.

8 Domaine National du Palais-Royal

This former royal palace (p107), originally called the Palais-Cardinal,

now houses State offices. It was built by Cardinal Richelieu in 1632, passing to the Crown on his death 10 years later, and was the childhood home of Louis XIV. The dukes of Orléans acquired it in the 18th century.

9 La Sorbonne

The city's great university (p133) had humble beginnings in 1253 as a college for 16 poor students to study theology. France's first printing house was also established here in 1469. After suppression during the Revolution, it became the University of Paris.

10 Palais du Luxembourg

L6 **15 Rue de Vaugirard, 75006** **For reserved group tours only; gardens: dawn–dush daily** **senat.fr**

Marie de Médici had architect Salomon de Brosse model this palace after her childhood home, the Pitti Palace in Florence. Shortly after its completion she was exiled by her son, Louis XIII. It was seized from the Crown during the Revolution to become a prison and now houses the French Senate. Book ahead for guided tours.

Spectacular gilded interiors of the Palais du Luxembourg

PLACES OF WORSHIP

The Chapel of the Virgin at the Église St-Eustache

Hôtel des Invalides *(p46)* complex – a monument in French Classical style. Built as the chapel for the resident soldiers of the Invalides, its ornate high altar starkly contrasts the solemn marble chapels surrounding the crypt, which hold the tombs of French military leaders.

6 The Panthéon
Modelled on the Pantheon in Rome, this domed late 18th-century church *(p42)* only served as a house of worship for two years, before becoming a monument and burial place for the great and the good of the Revolution era. Later, distinguished citizens were also buried here.

7 La Madeleine
📍 D3 🏛 Pl de la Madeleine, 75008
🕘 9:30am–7pm daily 🌐 lamadeleine paris.fr
Designed in the style of a Greek temple in 1764, this prominent church, surrounded by 52 Corinthian columns, was consecrated to Mary Magdalene in 1845. The bronze doors, which include bas-reliefs of the Ten Commandments, and the Last Judgment on the south pediment, are exterior highlights, while the ornate marble and gold interior has many fine statues, including François Rude's *Baptism of Christ*. It's also a popular venue for classical concerts. Note that timings for services vary.

1 Église St-Eustache
For centuries, this Gothic edifice *(p87)* was the market church serving the traders of Les Halles. Taking more than 100 years to build, it was finally completed in 1637 and its cavernous interior displays the architectural style of the early Renaissance. Popular Sunday afternoon organ recitals and other classical concerts take place in this wonderfully atmospheric setting.

2 Notre-Dame
The geographical "heart" of France, this Gothic cathedral *(p30)* is a repository of art and history.

3 Sacré-Coeur
This limestone basilica *(p36)* is adorned with a stunning mosaic and stained-glass windows. Its dome offers some of the finest views of Paris.

4 Sainte-Chapelle
Although this chapel *(p44)* is no longer used for worship, the stained-glass windows encourage reverence.

5 Église du Dôme
The final resting place of Napoleon Bonaparte is the Dôme Church in the

Baptism of Christ,
La Madeleine

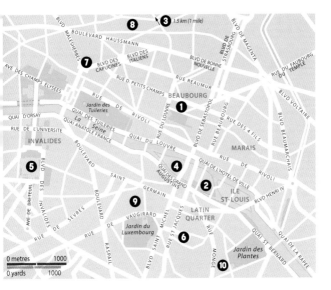

8 Grande Synagogue de la Victoire

E2 **44 Rue de la Victoire, 75009** **For group tours only** **lavictoire. org**

Built in the late 19th century, this elaborate synagogue is the second largest in Europe. The building is open only to those wishing to attend services and to groups who have arranged a visit in advance. Other smaller synagogues can be found in the Marais, which has long had a large Jewish community, including one at 10 Rue Pavée, built in 1913 by Hector Guimard, the architect who designed the city's magnificent Art Nouveau metro stations. Group tours take place in the mornings on weekdays.

9 Église St-Sulpice

Outstanding frescoes in the Chapel of the Angels by Eugène Delacroix are the highlight of this 17th-century church (p133). With more than 6,500 pipes, its organ, designed by Jean-François Chalgrin in 1776, is one of the largest in the world. The novelist Victor Hugo married his childhood sweetheart Adèle Foucher here in 1822.

10 Grande Mosquée de Paris

The city's Grand Mosque (p144) was built during the 1920s as a tribute to North African Muslims who offered military support to France during World War I. Its beautiful Moorish architecture, including a minaret, was executed by craftspeople brought over from North Africa. There's a shaded interior courtyard where visitors can sit and sip a glass of mint tea.

Tranquil, tiled gardens of the Grande Mosquée de Paris

MUSEUMS

Muséum National d'Histoire Naturelle surrounded by beautiful gardens

1 Muséum National d'Histoire Naturelle

Paris's Natural History Museum in the Jardin des Plantes *(p143)* contains a fascinating collection of animal skeletons, plant fossils, minerals and gemstones. Its highlight is the magnificent Grande Galerie de l'Évolution, which depicts the changing interaction between humankind and nature during the evolution of life on Earth.

2 Musée de l'Armée

Part of the Hôtel des Invalides complex relating to the military history of France, this museum *(p127)* has a huge number of military objects from the Middle Ages to World War II.

The collection includes armour, artillery, weapons, uniforms and paintings. Admission includes entrance to the Dôme Church, containing the tomb of Napoleon Bonaparte.

3 Musée des Arts Décoratifs

Set over nine levels, adjoining the west end of the Louvre's Richelieu Wing, this arts museum *(p106)* showcases furniture and tableware from the 12th century to the present day. The breathtaking anthology of pieces ranges from Gothic panelling and Renaissance porcelain to 1970s carpets and chairs by Philippe Starck. Also part of the museum is the Musée de la Mode et du Textile, which hosts fashion exhibitions, and the Musée de la Publicité, which has exhibitions on advertising.

4 Musée du Louvre

French and Italian sculpture, Greek and Roman antiquities and paintings from the 12th to the 19th centuries are just some of the highlights of the world's largest museum *(p22)*.

5 Musée du Cluny-Musée National du Moyen Age

This remarkable museum *(p134)* dedicated to the art of the Middle

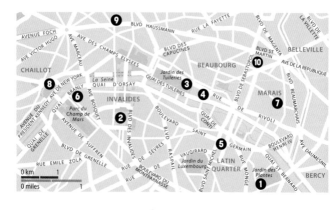

Medieval architecture at the Cité de l'Architecture et du Patrimoine

Ages is known by several names. This includes the Musée de Cluny, after the beautiful mansion in which it is housed, and the Thermes de Cluny, after the Roman baths adjoining the museum. Highlights include the famous *Lady and the Unicorn* tapestries, medieval stained glass, and exquisite gold crowns and jewellery.

6 Musée du Quai Branly – Jacques Chirac

In a city dominated by Western art, this fabulous museum *(p128)* tips the balance in favour of arts from Africa, Asia, Oceania and the Americas. Must-sees include the African instruments. The striking Jean Nouvel-designed building is an attraction in itself.

7 Musée Carnavalet

The vast collection at this museum *(p96)*, refurbished in 2021, charts the history of Paris. The museum occupies two adjoining mansions – Carnavalet and Le Peletier de St-Fargeau – both decorated with gilded wood panelling, furniture and objets d'art, including paintings and sculptures of famous personalities, and engravings showing the creation of Paris.

8 Cité de l'Architecture et du Patrimoine

The Cité de l'Architecture *(p121)* and the Musée des Monuments Français showcase French architectural heritage and form one of the world's foremost architectural centres. The Galerie des Moulages has models of French cathedrals.

9 Musée Jacquemart-André

Set in a private mansion, this museum *(p115)* was once the home of Edouard André and his artist wife Nélie Jacquemart. It houses their personal art collection, which features works by Boucher, Botticelli, Rembrandt and Fragonard, as well as excellent temporary exhibits.

10 Musée des Arts et Métiers

📍 G3 🏛 60 Rue Réaumur, 75003
🕐 10am–6pm Tue–Sun (to 9pm Fri)
🚫 1 Jan, 1 May, 25 Dec 🌐 arts-et-metiers.net 🔗

Housed in the medieval Abbaye de St-Martin-des-Champs, this industrial design museum is a fascinating repository of printing machines, vintage cars, music boxes, early flying machines, automatons and other inventions.

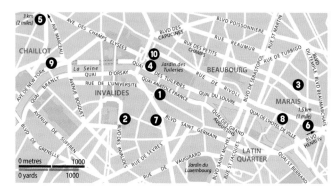

ART GALLERIES

1 Musée d'Orsay
This former railway station (p26) is one of the world's leading art galleries; the Impressionist works are a highlight.

2 Musée Rodin
Head to the gardens of the Musée Rodin (p128) to enjoy some of the French sculptor's most famous works, including *The Thinker* and *The Burghers of Calais*, while strolling among the shady trees and rose bushes. Auguste Rodin (1840–1917) lived and worked for nine years in the beautiful 18th-century Hôtel Biron, where the rest of the collection is housed. The elegant interiors contain some of Rodin's best-known works such as *The Kiss*, as well as artworks that he collected.

3 Musée Picasso
The beautiful Hôtel Salé (p40) showcases artworks by the famous Spanish-born artist Pablo Picasso.

4 Musée de l'Orangerie
🗺 D3 🚇 Jardin des Tuileries, 75001 🕐 9am–6pm Wed–Mon 🚫 1 May, 14 Jul (am), 25 Dec 🌐 musee-orangerie.fr 🔗

The prime exhibits here are eight of Monet's waterlily canvases, most of them painted between 1899 and 1921, and the gallery, located in a corner of the Tuileries (p106). The Walter-Guillaume collection covers works by Matisse, Picasso, Modigliani and other modern masters from 1870 to 1930.

5 Fondation Louis Vuitton
🗺 8 Ave du Mahatma Gandhi, Bois de Boulogne, 75116 🕐 Hours vary, check website 🌐 fondationlouis vuitton.fr 🔗

Close to the Jardin d'Acclimatation in the Bois de Boulogne (p160), Frank Gehry's dramatic glass structure was designed to evoke light and movement with panels of curved glass. Inside, it features a gallery and event space for concerts, performances and film screenings. Every year, the foundation curates two temporary exhibitions that focus on modern and contemporary art. Past

The Thinker,
Musée Rodin

exhibits have focused on the likes of Icelandic-Danish artist Olafur Eliasson, American artist Jean-Michel Basquiat and Frank Gehry himself.

6 Atelier des Lumières

📍 38 Rue Saint-Maur, 75011
🕐 10am–6pm daily (to 10pm Fri & Sat, 7pm Sun) 🗓 Jan & Feb
🌐 atelier-lumieres.com

Located in a restored 19th-century foundry in the Bastille area, this digital art centre uses 140 video projectors and a spatial sound system to create immersive digital art exhibitions. Watch the static paintings come to life, projected across an impressive 3,345 sq m (36,000 sq ft) space.

7 Musée Maillol

Works of the famous French artist Aristide Maillol, including his paintings and sculptures, are the focal point of this museum (p135), which was created by his model, Dina Vierny (1919–2009). Temporary exhibitions feature other artists, including Gustav Klimt, Keith Haring and Frida Kahlo.

8 Maison Européenne de la Photographie

If you're a photography fan, be sure not to miss this splendid gallery (p97) located in the Marais. Its exhibitions range from portraits to documentary work, retrospectives to contemporary photographers.

9 Palais de Tokyo

📍 B4 📍 13 Ave du Président Wilson, 75116 🕐 Noon–10pm Mon, Wed-Sun (to midnight Thu)
🌐 palaisdetohyo.com

Dedicated to contemporary art, this lively museum in the Chaillot area hosts regularly changing exhibitions and installations by international artists. It is one of the most cutting-edge art houses in Europe and has a bookshop, two restaurants and a nightclub (YoYo).

10 Jeu de Paume

📍 D3 📍 1 Pl de la Concorde, 75008 🕐 11am-7pm Wed-Sun (to 9pm Tue) 🗓 1 Jan, 1 May, 25 Dec
🌐 jeudepaume.org

This gallery is a fine exhibition space, set within a former 19th-century royal tennis court (jeu de paume), which is located in the Jardin des Tuileries (p105). It has a strong reputation for show-casing outstanding photography, film and video installations from the 20th and 21st centuries. The gallery also has a café with an outdoor terrace, which offers views of the garden and the Place de la Concorde (p105).

Artworks on display at the Jeu de Paume

RIVERFRONT SIGHTS

1 Eiffel Tower
Although the top of the Eiffel Tower *(p34)* can be seen above rooftops across the city, one of the best views of this Paris landmark is from the Seine. The Pont d'Iéna lies at the foot of the tower, bridging the river to link it to the Trocadéro Gardens *(p123)*. The tower, illuminated at night, is a highlight of a dinner cruise on the Seine.

2 Palais de Chaillot
The curved arms of the Palais de Chaillot *(p121)* encircling the Trocadéro Gardens can be seen from the Seine. In the centre of the gardens, magnificent fountains spout from the top of a long pool lined with statues, while two huge water cannons spray their charges back towards the river and the Eiffel Tower on the opposite bank.

3 Liberty Flame
🅿 C3
A replica of the New York Statue of Liberty's torch was erected here in 1987 by the *International Herald Tribune* to mark their centenary and honour the freedom fighters of the French Resistance during World War II. It is located on the right bank of the Pont de l'Alma, the bridge over the tunnel where Diana, Princess of Wales, was fatally injured in a car crash in 1997. The Liberty Flame has now become her unofficial memorial and is often draped with notes and flowers laid in her honour.

4 Grand Palais and Petit Palais
Gracing either side of the Pont Alexandre III are these two exhibition halls *(p113)*, built for the Universal Exhibition of 1900. The iron Art Nouveau skeleton of the Grand Palais is topped by an enormous glass roof, which is impressive when illuminated at night. The Petit Palais is smaller but similar in style, with a dome and many Classical features. The Grand Palais is closed for renovations until 2025, but a temporary replacement site – hosting similar exhibitions and events – has been built on the Champ de Mars.

5 Pont Alexandre III
The most beautiful bridge *(p114)* in Paris, the Pont Alexandre III is a riot of Art Nouveau decoration including cherubs, wreaths, lamps and other elaborate statuary. Built for the Universal Exhibition of 1900, it leads to the Grand Palais and Petit Palais.

Eiffel Tower and the Seine, viewed from Pont Alexandre III

There are wonderful views of the Invalides complex and the Champs-Élysées from the bridge.

6 Dôme Church

An impressive view of the Église de Dôme in the Hôtel des Invalides (p46) complex can be had from the Pont Alexandre III. The golden dome beckons visitors down the long parkway lined with streetlamps and statues.

7 Musée du Louvre

This grand museum (p22) stretches along the river from the Pont Royal to the Pont des Arts. The Denon Wing, which can be seen from the Seine, was largely built during the reigns of Henri IV and Louis XIII in the late 16th and early 17th centuries.

8 Notre-Dame

The great cathedral, although damaged (p30), is still majestic when viewed from the Left Bank of the Seine. It rises at the eastern end of the Île de la Cité above the remains of the ancient tribes who first settled Paris in the 3rd century BCE.

9 Musée d'Orsay

The view of this stunning art gallery (p26) from the Right Bank of the Seine is one of its finest angles, showing the arched terminals, clock faces and grand façade of this former railway station, built in 1898–1900.

Giant Baroque clock in the main hall of the Musée d'Orsay

Architect Victor Laloux designed it to harmonize with the Louvre and Tuileries Quarter across the river.

10 Conciergerie

This huge and imposing building (p81), which served as a notorious prison during the French Revolution, commands the western end of the Île de la Cité. The magnificent building retains some of its medieval features on the island, including a torture chamber, kitchens, a clock and the twin towers that rise above the Quai de l'Horloge.

PARKS AND GARDENS

1 Jardin des Tuileries
Now officially part of the Louvre, these gardens *(p105)* were laid out in the 17th century as part of the old Palais de Tuileries. They stretch along the Seine between the Louvre and Place de la Concorde. The walkways are lined with lime and chestnut trees. Statues include bronze figures by Aristide Maillol.

2 Jardin des Plantes
Established as a medicinal herb garden for the king in 1635, these vast botanical gardens *(p143)* are a wonderfully tranquil spot. Paths are lined with statuary and mature trees and there are some glasshouses, including one devoted to the flora of Nouvelle Caledonie.

3 Bois de Boulogne
On the weekends, Parisians head for this park *(p160)* on the western edge of the city, which has a boating lake and paths for cycling, jogging and strolling. There are three formal gardens, lakes and waterfalls, and even two horse-racing tracks. It's a good spot for a break from the city bustle.

4 Jardin du Luxembourg
Parisians love this centrally located park *(p133)*, set around the Palais du Luxembourg. The sweeping terrace is a great place for people-watching, while locals sunbathe around the octagonal Grand Bassin or sail toy boats in the water. Statues are dotted throughout the grounds, and there is a café.

5 Bois de Vincennes
Another great escape from the city, this park *(p160)* is to the east of Paris what the Bois de Boulogne is to the west. A former royal hunting ground, it was landscaped in the 1860s. Now it features ornamental lakes, the beautiful Parc Floral *(p63)*, a zoo and a spring funfair.

6 Jardin du Palais-Royal
🚇 L1 🏛 8 Rue Montpensier, 75001
These lovely gardens are enclosed by the 18th-century arcades of the Domaine National du Palais-Royal *(p107)*. Modern sculptures include Daniel Buren's controversial striped columns.

7 Parc Clichy-Batignolles
🏛 147 Rue Cardinet, 75017
A relaxed, neighbourhood feel characterizes this park in the heart of the laid-back Batignolles district. It was developed with an eye to ecology and biodiversity. Locals come to skate, play *pétanque*, tend the community gardens and laze on the lawns, while wildlife and rare flora thrive in the wetlands-like environment.

A pond flanked by Corinthian columns at Parc Monceau

8 Parc Monceau

The most fashionable green space in Paris, full of well-heeled residents of the nearby mansions and apartments. The lush landscaping dates from the 18th century, and some architectural follies, such as the Classical colonnade, survive.

9 Parc Montsouris

🚇 2 Rue Gazan, 75014

Located south of Montparnasse, this large park in central Paris was laid out in the English style, atop an old granite quarry, by landscape architect Adolphe Alphand between 1865 and 1878. Ernest Hemingway and other writers and artists frequented the park in the mid-20th century. It has a jogging path, lake and a bandstand.

10 Parc des Buttes-Chaumont

🚇 1–7 Rue Botzaris, 75019 🕐 Sep–Apr: 7am–8pm daily; May–Aug: 7am–10pm Mon–Fri, 24 hours Sat & Sun

Baron Haussmann created this retreat northeast of the city centre in 1867, from what was formerly a rubbish dump. His architects built artificial cliffs, waterfalls, streams and a lake complete with an island crowned by a Roman-style temple. There are fantastic views of the city from this hilly park. In the eastern part of the park is a trendy bar, Rosa Bonheur, which is open until late.

The expansive Jardin du Luxembourg in front of the stately palace

TOP 10
FOUNTAINS

1. Observatory Fountain
🗺 L6 🏛 Jardin du Luxembourg
A monumental bronze statue features four figures, representing the continents, that hold aloft a globe and are surrounded by horses at the base.

2. Four Seasons Fountain
🗺 C4 🏛 Rue de Grenelle
Paris in female form looks down on figures representing the Seine and Marne rivers, designed in 1739 by sculptor Edmé Bouchardon.

3. Fontaine des Innocents
Carved by Jean Goujon in 1547, the remarkable Fontaine des Innocents (p88) is Paris's oldest Renaissance fountain.

4. Medici Fountain
🗺 L6 🏛 Jardin du Luxembourg
Built for Marie de Médici, the ornate Medici Fountain is one of the most beautiful fountains in Paris.

5. Molière Fountain
🗺 E3 🏛 Rue de Richelieu
This 19th-century fountain honours the French playwright.

6. Agam Fountain
🏛 La Défense
Architect Yaacov Agam designed this fountain of water and lights, which is set in front of the Grand Arche.

7. Châtelet Fountain
🗺 N3 🏛 Pl du Châtelet
The two sphinxes of this 1808 fountain commemorate Napoleon's campaign in Egypt.

8. Stravinsky Fountain
🗺 P2 🏛 Rue Brisemiche
Representing the works of Russian composer Igor Stravinsky, this fountain features colourful sculptures, spinning and spraying water.

9. Trocadéro Fountains
Spouting towards the Eiffel Tower, these fountains (p123) are illuminated at night.

10. Versailles Fountains
The fountains at Versailles (p159) flow to music at weekends in spring and summer.

OFF THE BEATEN TRACK

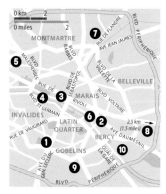

balconies (not to mention smart interiors) are a treat to see close up.

3 Little-visited Louvre

While many flock to the *Mona Lisa* and *Venus de Milo*, canny visitors set out to discover other parts of the Louvre's collections (p22), such as the Islamic arts section. It includes beautiful Iznik tiles and exquisite glass, gold and ivory objects from Andalusia, Iraq and India – all under a stunning gold filigree roof.

4 Canal Barge Cruise

J2 12 Port de Solferino, 75007 Cruise dates vary, chech website pariscanal.com

A great way to see a different side of Paris is to take a barge along the Seine, the Marne river and Canal St-Martin. Some Paris canal boats, for example, depart from the quay outside the Musée d'Orsay (p26) and make their way westwards to the island of Chatou, once frequented by Impressionist painters, or eastwards past Notre-Dame to Chennevières-sur-Marne, a favourite haunt of Pissaro.

1 Catacombs

1 Ave du Colonel Henri Rol-Tanguy, 75014 9:45am–8:30pm Tue–Sun 1 Jan, 1 May, 25 Dec catacombes.paris.fr

The catacombs are an underground warren of tunnels, filled with the bones of some six million Parisians, brought here from 1785 to 1865 as a solution to the problem of overflowing cemeteries. Aside from the macabre sight of walls lined with skulls and bones, it's a thrill to enter the tunnels, part of a vast quarry network that underlies the city. Limited numbers of visitors are allowed in at a time; pre-book a timed entry slot online.

2 Promenade Plantée

H5

Starting near the Opéra National de Paris Bastille (p96) and ending at Bois de Vincennes, this 4-km (2.5-mile) walkway, some of it high above the streets on a former railway viaduct, is a wonderful way to see a little-visited part of the city. Planted all along with trees and flowers, the path runs past tall mansion blocks, whose decorative mouldings and

A barge steadily cruising through Canal St-Martin

Ornate furnishings in the drawing room at the Musée Nissim de Camondo

5 Musée Nissim de Camondo

📍 C2 📍 63 Rue de Monceau, 75008 🕐 10am–5:30pm Wed–Sun 🌐 madparis.fr/Musee-Nissim-de-Camondo 🔗

Wealthy art collector Count Moïse de Camondo had this grand mansion built to house his superb collection of 18th-century art. The rooms are full of tapestries, paintings, gilded furniture and Sèvres porcelain. As interesting as the artworks is the portrait that emerges of a well-to-do family, beset by tragedy (it is named for his son, killed in World War I) and ultimately victim to Auschwitz.

6 Pavillon de l'Arsenal

📍 R5 📍 21 Blvd Morland, 75004 🕐 11am–7pm Tue–Sun 🌐 pavillon-arsenal.com

A museum dedicated to urban planning and architecture, the Pavillon de l'Arsenal is home to a small but fascinating exhibition illustrating the architectural evolution of Paris. Using film, models and panoramic photographs, it explores how the city has developed over the centuries and what future plans hold.

7 Le Centquatre-Paris

📍 5 Rue Curial, 75019 🕐 Noon–7pm Tue–Fri, 11am–7pm Sat & Sun 🌐 104.fr

The "104" is a huge arts centre, housed in a converted 19th-century funeral parlour with a lofty glass roof. It contains numerous artists' studios and workshops, and puts on excellent exhibitions and installations, as well as music, dance, cinema and theatre.

8 Parc Floral de Paris

📍 Route de la Pyramide, 75012 🕐 Summer: 9:30am–8pm daily (winter: to dusk) 🌐 parcfloraldeparis.com 🔗

Set within the Bois de Vincennes, this lovely park has wonderful displays of camellias, rhododendrons, ferns and irises. It hosts horticultural exhibitions and jazz concerts in summer and has plenty to appeal to children, including an adventure park. Visits to the park are free from October to March.

9 Buttes-aux-Cailles

The Butte-aux-Cailles quarter, in the southeast of the city, is a bit like a mini-Montmartre, with its pretty cobbled streets and old-fashioned streetlamps. The main Rue de la Butte-aux-Cailles with its restaurants and bohemian bars buzzes well into the night.

10 Bercy Village

📍 28 Rue François Truffaut, 75012 🌐 bercyvillage.com

The district of Bercy is where barges from all over France used to deliver wine to the capital. The former warehouses, a handsome ensemble of ochre-coloured stone buildings, have been converted into shops, restaurants and, fittingly, wine bars. It's well worth a wander, especially on Sundays when shops in most other parts of Paris are closed.

FAMILY ATTRACTIONS

1 Disneyland® Paris
The French offspring of America's favourite theme park (p159) is a clone of its parent, and features two parks, including the Walt Disney Studios® complex. There are rides for children of all ages and most adults are equally enchanted.

2 Musée de la Magie et des Automates
O R4 **O** 11 Rue St-Paul, 75004 **O** 2–7pm Wed, Sat, Sun (daily during school hols, except Jul & Aug) **W** museedelamagie. com

Kids will be thrilled by this museum of magic, located in the cellars of the former home of the Marquis de Sade. Magicians conjure up shows every half hour involving optical illusions, card tricks and lots of audience participation. Exhibits include working automata and memorabilia of magicians such as Houdini (1874–1926).

3 Parc Astérix
O Plailly, 60128 **O** Hours vary, chech website **W** parcasterix.fr

There's not just the Gaul of Asterix and Obelix to discover here, but six worlds, including ancient Greece and Rome, and all with the charm of Goscinny and Uderzo's beloved comic books. Dozens of attractions include one of Europe's longest roller coasters.

4 Jardin d'Acclimatation
O A2 **O** Bois de Boulogne, 75016 **O** 11am–6pm daily **W** jardind acclimatation.fr

Located at the north end of the Bois de Boulogne (p160), this amusement park is a big hit with children and features many attractions, such as roller coasters, pony rides and puppet shows. An electric train, "le Petit Train", runs to the park from Porte Maillot.

5 Eiffel Tower
A trip to the top is one of the most memorable activities for children in Paris (p34).

6 Grande Galerie de l'Evolution
The most imaginatively designed section in the Muséum National d'Histoire Naturelle (p143) is the Great Gallery of Evolution. Elephants, giraffes and other stuffed animals rise out of a recreated savannah, and a huge whale skeleton hangs from the ceiling, while special displays help tell the story of the development of life on Earth. Nature workshops are also held during school holidays.

7 Parc de la Villette
This is one of the top attractions for children (p160), with activities for all ages. The huge Cité des Sciences et de l'Industrie, a high-tech hands-on science museum, gets star billing, while the Cité des Enfants is a science and

**The electric train in the
Jardin d'Acclimatation**

nature attraction ideal for younger children. Kids can also admire the Argonaute, a real 1950s submarine that voyaged around the world 10 times and the Géode with its IMAX screen.

8 Musée des Arts Forains
📍 Pavillons de Bercy, 53 Ave des Terroirs de France, 75012
🕐 Hours vary, chech website
🌐 arts-forains.com 🚇🚻

This private museum, housed in a former wine warehouse in Bercy Village *(p63)*, is a secret wonderland filled with vintage fairground attractions, automata, theatre props, antique merry-go-rounds and a 1920s hall of mirrors. It is open by appointment for guided tours all year round, but visitors are welcome without prior reservations for 10 days over the Christmas and New Year period to try out the traditional fairground games and ride on the carousels.

9 Jardin du Luxembourg
A green oasis in the heart of the Left Bank, this *(p133)* is one of the most popular parks in Paris. It has tennis courts, puppet shows, donkey rides and a modern playground (for a fee). But most fun of all is the traditional Parisian pastime of sailing model boats in the octagonal Grand Bassin and riding the 19th-century carousel.

10 Parc des Buttes-Chaumont
The highest in Paris, this park *(p61)* is great for a family picnic. For many, this panoramic hilly site is the most pleasant park in the city. Kids enjoy exploring the rugged terrain with its lake, grassy slopes, suspended bridges and waterfalls, as well as pony rides and puppet shows. Le Pavillion du Lac and Rosa Bonheur are perfect spots for drinks.

TOP 10
MERRY-GO-ROUNDS

1. Jardin du Luxembourg
Children can play the traditional French game of rings on this historic 1879 merry-go-round.

2. Montmartre
At the foot of Sacré-Coeur *(p36)* is a grand double-decker merry-go-round.

3. Parc de la Villette
An aeroplane, a hot-air balloon and a Tintin-style space rocket join the wooden horses on this two-storey merry-go-round.

4. Jardin d'Acclimatation
A traditional carousel with wooden horses is just one of the collection of merry-go-rounds here.

5. Jardins du Trocadéro
A hot-air balloon graces this dual-platform merry-go-round *(p105)*.

6. Hôtel de Ville
Lucky riders jump on whenever this seasonal merry-go-round appears in the heart of the town.

7. Jardin des Plantes
The curious Dodo Manège *(p146)* features extinct animals including horned, giraffe-like sivatherium.

8. Parc Monceau
This charming little carousel *(p61)* is much loved by the local children.

9. Jardin des Tuileries
Set among the trees, antique wooden horses spin round this enchanting merry-go-round *(p105)*.

10. Eiffel Tower
The Parisian icon *(p104)* provides a dramatic backdrop to this solar-powered merry-go-round.

A carousel near the Eiffel Tower

NIGHTS OUT

1 Boat parties
During the day, the *peniches* (barges) moored along the Seine look peaceful, but after dark many of them become foot-stomping clubs. Rosa's *(Port des Invalides)* themed nights are great for dancing, while Marcounet *(Port des Célestins)* is the place for live music, with a vast terrace on land that makes it delightful during the summer.

2 Top-tier opera
Paris is home to a flourishing opera scene, with regular shows performed at both the opulent Palais Garnier *(p106)* and its modern sister venue, the Opéra National de Paris Bastille *(p96)*. More of a theatre buff? La Comédie Française *(1 Place Colette)* offers everything from modern shows to Molière revisited.

3 Museum lates
Paris has more museums than any other city in the world, and many of them keep their doors open late. The Fondation Louis Vuitton *(p56)* and the Bourse de Commerce *(p87)* all host late openings one day a week, while the Musée du Vin *(p123)* goes a step further, offering DJ sets on Friday nights.

4 Live music
Paris is a hub for live music. The Philharmonie de Paris *(philharmoniede paris.fr)* is a must for classical fans, while jazz-lovers are spoilt for choice, with spots like Au Duc des Lombards hosting regular shows. To discover the next big thing, check out the secret gigs schedule at Sofar Sounds *(sofarsounds.com)*, with pop-up locations across the city.

5 Clubs
It's not hard to find a spot in Paris to dance the night away. The ecclectic La Machine du Moulin Rouge *(lamachine dumoulinrouge.com)* pumps out everything from techno to '90s music night after night. Supersonic, just off Canal Saint-Martin, has (often free) performances of every rock genre imaginable, including post-rock, garage and punk.

6 Comedy
Belly laughs can be found in comedy clubs across Paris, but Olivier Giraud's one man show at the Théâtre des Nouveautés *(theatredesnouveautes. fr)* is a highlight. Performed in English, this hit show sees Giraud take the audience through situations they might encounter in Paris and how a local would react, for plenty of light-hearted, self-deprecating laughs.

7 Cabaret
Where better to see cabaret than in bohemian Montmartre, where it was born? Here, the iconic Moulin Rouge *(p152)* puts on spectacular shows. But don't miss the performances at

Paris's most famous cabaret club, the Moulin Rouge in Montmartre

Folies-Bergère (*foliesbergere.com*) either, which has been around since 1870 and has hosted some truly famous cabaret stars, notably Josephine Baker.

8 French cinema
Paris has plenty of options to tempt film lovers. In fact, it's home to the largest cinema in Europe, Le Grand Rex (*legrandrex.com*), which welcomes 2,800 viewers at once for new releases. For fans of the classic silver screen, there's the 1907 Cinéma du Panthéon (*13 Rue Victor Cousin*), the oldest cinema in Paris still in use, which showcases a mix of indie and older titles.

9 One-of-a-kind bars
Paris is home to countless cool rooftop bars, with the one at Hôtel Dame des Arts (*damedesarts.com*) offering views over Saint-Sulpice, Notre-Dame and the Eiffel Tower. If you're looking for something more historic, there's Harry's New York Bar (*harrysbar.com*), which has a big cocktail menu and a basement piano bar.

10 Evening Seine cruises
For a truly memorable evening, cruise along the Seine aboard one of the city's *bateaux mouches* (pleasure boats) or jump aboard the Ducasse sur Seine (*ducasse-seine.com*). Both offer dinner and drinks as you cruise past Paris's iconic landmarks, including the sparkling Eiffel Tower (*p34*).

A classical music performance at the Philharmonie de Paris

TOP 10
JAZZ CLUBS

1. Au Duc des Lombards
🗺 N2 🏠 42 Rue des Lombards
The best overseas jazz artists come here to play with homegrown talent, with more than 300 concerts a year.

2. New Morning
🗺 F2 🏠 7–9 Rue des Petites Ecuries
A truly eclectic mix of music, with plenty of jam sessions and impromptu performances.

3. Baiser Salé
🗺 N2 🏠 58 Rue des Lombards
Jazz, blues and World Music are the mainstays at this tiny cellar club.

4. Caveau des Oubliettes
🗺 F5 🏠 52 Rue Garlande
Jazz in an ex-dungeon, with free jam sessions on Tuesdays, Wednesdays, Thursdays and Sundays.

5. La Bellevilloise
🗺 F1 🏠 19–21 Rue Boyer
An alternative music venue in Belleville, which is a local favourite for live music.

6. Jazz Club Etoile
🗺 A2 🏠 81 Blvd Gouvion-St-Cyr
Features visiting musicians and has a jazzy brunch on Sunday.

7. Sunset-Sunside
🗺 N2 🏠 60 Rue des Lombards
A double serving of late-night jazz: acoustic and modern at street level; electric, fusion and groove in the cellar.

8. La Péniche Marcounet
🗺 Q4 🏠 Port des Célestins, Quai de l'Hôtel de ville, 75004
An old barge converted into a live jazz venue. Its Sunday jazz brunch has become very popular.

9. Le Petit Journal St-Michel
🗺 M5 🏠 71 Blvd St-Miche
New Orleans-style swinging jazz in a lively Latin Quarter cellar.

10. Caveau de la Huchette
🗺 N4 🏠 5 Rue de la Huchette
This compact little club has been hosting jazz performances for over 70 years.

FRENCH CUISINE

A plate laden with a croque monsieur, a ham-and-cheese toasted sandwich

1 Croque monsieur

Roughly translating as "gentleman's crunch", the croque monsieur is a classic. A toasted sandwich made with ham and cheese, it's served in cafés and boulangeries around the city, including at La Fontaine de Belleville (lafontaineparis.fr).

2 Boeuf bourguignon

Like so many dishes that France now counts among haute-cuisine, boeuf bourguignon was once the food of the poor, a way of slow cooking old, tough chunks of steak to make them appetizing. It first originated in the Burgundy region, it's now a staple in bistros across Paris. Try it at Lapérouse (p141), which serves a recipe unchanged for generations.

3 Suprême de volaille

A piece of chicken breast might not sound special, but suprême de volaille dresses up this basic ingredient. While there's no set way of cooking the chicken – you can find the dish poached, roasted or sautéed – it's often accompanied by a rich, wine-heavy sauce. Le Coq & Fils (p157) is great, but you'll find the dish on many bistro menus.

4 Oysters

Paris might not be a city by the sea, but that doesn't stop it being a fantastic place to enjoy seafood – especially oysters, which are seen as a luxurious delicacy here. The dish is often served at celebrations like Christmas and New Year, but many a Parisian can be found enjoying a plate come lunchtime at the likes of Au Pied de Cochon (p93), with a glass of white wine in hand.

5 Confit de canard

Sometimes simple dishes are best, and that's certainly the case with confit de canard. Here, a duck leg is salted and cooked in its own fat for at least two hours, after which the drumstick is then covered with the fat again and put in jars to store. It's usually served cold or at room temperature, often with extra crispy roast potatoes on the side. Plenty of spots across Paris offer this dish, but Art Deco Thoumieux (p131) tops the lot.

6 Fondue

Parisians join in the scrum to claim fondue – most often associated with the Alps – as their own as soon as winter arrives, with restaurants like Le Refuge des Fondus (lerefugedesfondus.com) serving up delicious options. A classic recipe includes the ABC of cheese (Abondance, Beaufort and Comté), mixed with white wine and garlic, and typically served with bread from the day before.

A restaurant table in Paris laden with fondue

Enjoying a variety of delicious buckwheat galettes

7 Galettes

Originally from Brittany, these dark, buckwheat crêpes are very popular in Paris. They come in sweet and savoury varieties, but the most typical is the *complète*, which is filled with ham, egg and cheese. For a menu full of choice, try La Crêperie du Manoir Breton *(18 Rue d'Odessa)*, or if you're after decadent dessert crêpes, make for the award-winning Breizh Café *(p103)*.

8 Steak-frites

It's hard to find a classic Parisian bistro that doesn't feature steak-frites on its menu. This simple yet comforting dish of steak and chips is wildly popular in Paris, although be aware that steak is often served on the rarer side. A meat lover's paradise, Au Petit Marguery *(p147)* is a great place to sample it.

9 Gigot d'agneau

Thought to have originated with the Romans, who would slow cook lamb all night long, *gigot d'agneau* is a roasted lamb's leg often made with Provençal herbs like rosemary and thyme. While many restaurants reserve this dish for special occasions, such as Easter, Sébillon *(sebillon.com)* has it year round.

10 Crème brûlée

Made from eggs and cream, and topped with a layer of burnt sugar, this rich dish has been gracing recipe books since the 17th century. It's regularly featured on set menus, or in miniature form as part of a *café gourmand* (a selection of mini desserts served with an espresso). Pint-sized Le Hangar *(p93)* is famed for its desserts, and almost always has crème brûlée on the menu.

TOP 10
BOULANGERIE AND PATISSERIE BUYS

1. Baguette tradition
Left to rise for longer, these delicious baguettes have a crunchier crust than a regular baguette.

2. Pain au chocolat
A classic French pastry that's flaky, buttery and filled with chocolate.

3. Macarons
With sweet buttercream wedged between two meringue biscuits, macarons come in every colour and flavour imaginable.

4. Madeleines
These buttery shell-shaped cakes are a popular snack for children.

5. Tarte aux pommes
Made with fruit from the likes of Normandy and Brittany, these apple tarts are a French classic.

6. Eclairs
Indulgent choux pastry filled with cream and topped with chocolate.

7. Jambon-beurre
This classic ham-and-butter sandwich, often the cheapest available from bakeries, is served on baguette bread.

8. Galette des rois
This marzipan, flaky pastry tart is often eaten around Epiphany (6 January), but is available throughout the month at bakeries.

9. Tarte au citron meringuée
Tangy lemon combines with soft meringue and shortcrust pastry to make this pie.

10. Paris-Brest
Crown shaped and cream filled, this pastry was created to commemorate the Paris–Brest bicycle race in 1910.

A delicious Paris-Brest

CAFÉS AND BARS

1 Café de Flore
A popular hangout for artists and intellectuals since the 1920s, Café de Flore (p139) attracted regulars including Salvador Dalí and Albert Camus. During World War II Jean-Paul Sartre and Simone de Beauvoir more or less lived at the Flore. Although its prices have skyrocketed since then, its charming Art Deco decor hasn't changed and it's still a favourite with French filmmakers and literati. Its reliably delicious coffee is best enjoyed at an outside table.

2 Le Progrès
Don't be fooled by the fairly unremarkable exterior of this Parisian bar and café (p102). Inside, an eclectic mix of locals congregate to people-watch and catch up with friends, always with a drink in hand. Wood panelling and chalkboards give the café a truly authentic, old-world feel.

3 Café Marly
Overlooking the courtyard of the Louvre, this café (p109) is as sleek as the former palace is regal. From morning coffee to evening wine, Café Marly is the place to rest in between visits to the museum. While it is a far cry from the usual corner café, the experience is justifiably royal thanks to its plush interior and velvet armchairs.

4 Carette
This pavement café (p103), situated just around the corner from the Jardins du Trocadéro, is the perfect setting for lunch. French staples line the menu, and they serve an excellent Sunday brunch. Find a table on the terrace for an exemplary croque monsieur or one of the picture-perfect pastries.

5 Les Deux Magots
This café (p139) was a rival to the neighbouring Flore as a rendezvous for the 20th-century intellectual elite. Ernest Hemingway, Oscar Wilde, Djuna

Outdoor seating at Les Deux Magots on Boulevard St-Germain

Barnes, André Breton and Paul Verlaine were all regulars. Picasso also met his muse Dora Maar here in 1937. Like many iconic Parisian cafés, Les Deux Magots is pricey, but the outside tables facing the boulevard and square – ideally experienced with a glass of fizz – are definitely worth the price tag.

6 La Closerie des Lilas
The main restaurant here (p165) is expensive, but the bar is a good spot to soak up the atmosphere of this historic site, founded in 1847, where artists and writers such as Georges Braque and Gertrude Stein once came to mingle. Look out for the famous names of visitors etched on the tables in the bar. The outdoor seating makes for a lovely, leafy setting in summer. The busy brasserie also has live piano music in the evenings and attracts a chic crowd.

7 Café de la Paix
This spot (p109) can be found along one of Haussmann's grand boulevards,

and has views of the opulent Palais Garnier (p106). This setting makes it hard to contest the pricier coffee served inside. The café is decked floor to ceiling with decor typical of the Napoleon III style, making it a historic monument. Sip drinks and discuss current affairs just like Maupassant or Zola would have in the 19th century.

8 Le Procope

Also known as Café Procope, this establishment (p139) was founded in 1686, making it the oldest café in Paris. During its heyday in the Age of Enlightenment, it attracted influential French philosophers, writers and leaders such as Rousseau and Voltaire. Expect traditional French classics like escargots and foie gras, served in an atmospheric space complete with art-hung walls and glittering chandeliers.

9 Caffè Stern

Originally a 19th-century engraving workshop, Caffè Stern (p109) is now an Italian café. It is popular for its robust coffee, especially its custom blend, which is made by the artisan Italian coffee roaster Gianni Frasi at the Laboratorio Torrefazione Giamaica in Verona. In the kitchen, chef Denis Mattiuzzi serves up dishes like Venetian veal liver with fried polenta and dill taglioni with lobster, squid and pistachio sauce.

10 Le Relais de la Butte

The terrace in front of this unassuming café (p157), located high up in Montmartre, is one of Paris's best outdoor theatres. Locals pass the evening watching the sun set over the city as the lights begin to sparkle. The food and drink play second fiddle to the experience of sitting in this little leafy enclave, which in the summer is always busy. Montmartre is laden with watering holes of varying quality, but Le Relais de la Butte is always a sure bet, as long as the weather cooperates.

TOP 10 WINE BARS

1. La Belle Hortense
G4 31 Rue Vieille du Temple 01 48 04 71 60
A wine bar that doubles as a bookshop.

2. L'Avant Comptoir de la Terre
M5 3 Carrefour de l'Odéon
camdeborde.com
Jostle around the zinc bar for delicious little bites and glasses of natural wine.

3. Frenchie Bar à Vins
F3 6 Rue du Nil
frenchie-bav.com
A superb international wine list.

4. Le Barav
R1 6 Rue Charles-François Dupuis lebarav.fr
Well-priced wines in the upper Marais.

5. Le Garde Robe
M2 41 Rue de l'Arbre Sec
legarderobe.net
Cheeses, oysters and charcuterie round out the menu of natural wines here.

6. Septime La Cave
3 Rue Basfroi septime-lacave.fr
Quaint wine store of Septime (p103).

7. Verjus Bar à Vins
E3 47 Rue Montpensier
verjusparis.com
This cosy wine bar specializes in independent French winemakers.

8. Déviant
F2 39 Rue des Petites Écuries deviant.paris
Natural wines pair with small plates here.

9. Le Baron Rouge
An unpretentious, long-time favourite (p103) near the Aligre market that serves fresh oysters when in season.

10. Quedubon
H2 22 Rue du Plateau
restaurantquedubon.fr
A list of over 200 natural wines.

SHOPS AND MARKETS

Marais from the Bastille. Sunday is the best day, when locals come to socialize as well as shop for fish, meat, bread and cheese. Some stalls sell North African and other international food.

4 Place de la Madeleine
This is a gourmand's delight (p106). Some of the most delectable speciality food shops in Paris are dotted around the edges of this square, including the famous Fauchon food hall. There's Maille for mustard, Kaspia for caviar, Marquise de Sévigné for chocolates and La Maison de la Truffe (p108) for truffles. Several elegant *salons de thé* offer a spot to sit and sip too.

5 Galeries Lafayette
E2 **40 Blvd Haussmann, 75009**
This expansive store opened in 1894 as a monument to Parisian style, topped by a glorious steel-and-glass dome.

1 Marché aux Fleurs Reine Elizabeth II
P4 **Pl Louis-Lépine, 75004**
Dating from 1808, the colourful Marché aux Fleurs Reine Elizabeth II (p32) on the Île de la Cité is the oldest and one of the largest flower markets in Paris. Its blooms – everything from orchids to orange trees – brighten up the area between the stark walls of the Conciergerie and Hôtel Dieu from Monday to Saturday.

2 Printemps
E2 **64 Blvd Haussmann, 75009**
One of Paris's top department stores, the iconic Printemps opened in 1864. Its goods range from designer clothing and accessories to mid-range labels and funky fashions, home decor and furniture. The sixth-floor brasserie is crowned with a lovely Art Nouveau stained-glass cupola.

3 Bastille Market
H5 **Blvd Richard-Lenoir, 75011**
Every Thursday and Sunday morning, this market stretches along the tree-lined boulevard that separates the

The spectacular steel-and-glass domed ceiling of Galeries Lafayette

Stalls selling fresh produce at the bustling Marché d'Aligre

Along with designer clothes, there's a fabulous food hall. The seventh floor has great views.

6 Merci
Featuring homeware, clothing, furniture and a range of curated design products, Merci *(p100)* is a playful alternative to traditional department stores. After a spot of shopping, visit the canteen on the kitchen level or grab a coffee at the charming ground-floor café. It's the place to shop and be seen just north of the Marais.

7 Rue Mouffetard
One of the oldest market streets *(p144)* in Paris winds downhill through the Latin Quarter every morning Tuesday to Sunday. Although this formerly budget-friendly and bohemian market has been discovered as a tourist spot, it retains its charm, the narrow streets lined with speciality shops. There are also some good restaurants in the quieter side streets.

8 Marché d'Aligre
🚇 H5 🏠 Pl d'Aligre, 75012
Away from the tourist bustle, this market preserves its authentic Parisian atmosphere. An indoor hall houses vendors selling cheese, artisan beer, olive oil and charcuterie among other high-quality goods. Outside, inexpensive fruit, vegetables and flowers fill the street-side stands every morning from Tuesday to Sunday.

9 Marché aux Puces de St-Ouen
🏠 Porte de Clignancourt, 75018
Every Saturday to Monday the largest antiques market in the world is held here. There are actually several markets here: the oldest, Marché Vernaison, is the most charming featuring antiques, knick-knacks, linens and decor items. Marché Biron offers a wide range of art, fine furniture, interesting jewellery and paintings.

10 Le Bon Marché
🚇 D5 🏠 24 Rue de Sèvres, 75007
Paris's first department store was founded on the Left Bank in 1852, its structure partially designed by Gustave Eiffel *(p35)*. Today it's even more hip than its competitors, with an in-store boutique featuring avant-garde fashions. It also has designer clothes, its own line of menswear as well as the enormous La Grande Épicerie food hall.

PARIS FOR FREE

1 Place des Vosges
Originally named Place Royale, this exceptionally beautiful arcaded square (*p95*) dating to 1605 is a peaceful area to stroll and sit. The Classical arcades contain many art galleries. At No 6, the Maison de Victor Hugo is the former dwelling of the famous writer and contains a museum dedicated to his life. The permanent collections are free.

2 Cinéma en Plein Air
◊ Prairie du Triangle, 75019
ⓦ lavillette.com

Each summer a giant screen is placed in Parc de la Villette (*p160*), showing movies (in the original language, with French subtitles) in the open air every evening for a month. The films range from classics to the less well known and are free. Deckchairs and blankets are available for hire, and many people bring their own picnic to make an evening of it.

3 Petit Palais
The grand Neo-Classical Petit Palais (*p114*) is anything but "little", and is home to the Musée des Beaux Arts de la Ville de Paris (*p114*), a fascinating collection of art and artifacts, including some fine Art Nouveau pieces. There's a charming inner garden with a café too. Check the website for details about occasional free lunchtime concerts held in the auditorium.

4 Free Visits to Museums
Seize the opportunity to view the permanent collections of several museums, including the Musée Rodin (*p128, Oct–Mar*), Quai Branly (*p128*) and Musée d'Orsay (*p26*), for free on the first Sunday of every month. Arrive early to avoid the long queues.

5 Cimetière du Père Lachaise
It is easy to while away an entire afternoon at Père Lachaise Cemetery (*p161*), tracking down celebrity graves including those of Oscar Wilde, Colette, Balzac, Édith Piaf, Chopin and Jim Morrison. With its moss-grown tombs and ancient trees, it's also an atmospheric and romantic place for a long stroll.

Grave of Frédéric Chopin, Père Lachaise

A fountain in the centre of
Place des Vosges

6 Hôtel de Ville
Paris's grand city hall (p50) hosts regular excellent, free exhibitions, usually on a Parisian theme; a recent show focused on the Liberation of Paris. Free events often take place on the forecourt, but the wide square is just as fine a place to people-watch on any regular day.

7 Berges de Seine
B4–E4
The Berges de Seine, the stretch of river that runs between the Musée du Quai Branly – Jacques Chirac and Musée d'Orsay, is an attractive, lively promenade with plenty of free activities, such as concerts, workshops, board games, a climbing wall and play spaces for children. There's a riverfront walkway on the Right Bank too.

8 Les Journées du Patrimoine
journeesdupatrimoine.culture.fr
On the third weekend of September, many buildings that are usually off-limits, such as the Élysée Palace, are opened up to the public for free.

9 Musée d'Art Moderne de la Ville de Paris
This museum of modern art (p122), with a forecourt giving onto the Seine, may not rival the Pompidou's collection, but it's free and often offers a calmer atmosphere. Almost all of the major 20th-century artists who worked in France are represented, including Picasso, Braque, Chagall and Modigliani, along with some new modern artists.

10 Organ and Choir Recitals
Free organ recitals are given at 5pm on Sundays in the beautiful Église St-Eustache (p87), which has one of the finest organs in France. La Madeleine (p52) and Saint-Roch also host free classical music concerts.

TOP 10 BUDGET TIPS

A classic French breakfast

1. Out for breakfast
Having breakfast at a café will cost considerably less than at a hotel.

2. Youth savings
State-run museums, including the Louvre, are free for anyone under 18 and EU citizens under 26.

3. Set-price lunch
Fixed-price (prix fixe) lunches are usually good value and almost always cost less than evening meals.

4. Cutting transport costs
Buying a carnet of tickets, a Mobilis or Paris Visite card (p169) will save on transport costs.

5. Lodgings for less
It's almost always cheaper to stay in an apartment, B&B or hostel than at a hotel.

6. Cut-price entertainment
Same-day theatre and concert tickets are sold for half the price at kiosks on Place de la Madeleine (p107).

7. Order a carafe
A carafe of wine is better value than a bottle, and the house wine is generally very good.

8. Museum pass
With so many museums to visit, the Paris Museum Pass offers savings (parismuseumpass.com).

9. Sightseeing by bus
The bus is a great way of sightseeing affordably – for example, number 24 takes a scenic route along the Seine.

10. Cheaper movies
Cinema tickets in the 5th arrondissement (around the Panthéon) are cheaper than those elsewhere.

FESTIVALS AND EVENTS

1 Street Music
Parisians love to celebrate music. The Fête de la Musique (*fetedelamusique.culture.gouv.fr*), held on the summer equinox, is Paris's largest music festival, when amateur and professional musicians take to the streets. There are performances in Place de la République and concert venues, but the most fun is to be had wandering through neighbourhoods.

2 Garden Magic
During summer weekend evenings the gardens of Versailles (*chateauversailles-spectacles.fr*) are home to the Grandes Eaux Nocturnes. Superb illuminations and installations, plus a dazzling firework display over the Grand Canal, make this a midsummer night's dream.

3 All That Jazz
Paris has a long tradition of jazz, which was introduced to the city during World War I. A summer highlight is the Paris Jazz Festival (*festivalsduparcfloral.paris*). The Parc Floral in the Bois de Vincennes (*p160*)

is the main setting, blending a verdant backdrop with jazz melodies. Jazz à la Villette (*jazzalavillette.com*) in September takes place in the Cité de la Musique.

4 Film Screenings
Cinema is embedded in Paris's culture. The four-day Fête du Cinéma (*feteducinema.com*), held in early summer, allows film buffs to watch films at cinemas across Paris for just €4. The focus is on niche, independent movies.

5 City Beach
A popular summer event, Paris Plages (*paris.fr*) transforms a stretch of the Seine *quais* and the Canal du l'Ourcq into a mini Cannes, with deck chairs, parasols and palm trees.

6 Cycling Fun
Don't miss the Tour de France (*letour.fr*) if you want to understand the French passion for cycling. Held annually since 1903, the world's greatest and most gruelling cycle race approaches Paris after 23 days. On the final laps the riders pass the

Louvre, race along the banks of the Seine, hurtle down the Rue de Rivoli and cross the finish line on the Champs-Élysées.

7 Performing Arts
From plays and cabarets to music and dance, Paris stages a huge range of shows. For contemporary performing arts, head to the Festival d'Automne à Paris (festivalautomne.com). Founded in 1972, this festival encourages people from all walks of life to enjoy performances of dance, music, film and drama.

8 Avant-Garde Art
A leader in avant-garde art in the early 20th century, Paris continues its cutting-edge artistic legacy with the Nuit Blanche (parisinfo.com), first held here in 2002. This free all-night arts event in early June provides a fresh perspective on the city, with concerts, plays, installations and illuminations of famous landmarks.

9 Grape Harvest Celebrations
Paris was once a major wine producer but these days only the vineyards at Montmartre produce wine (p153), yielding just under a thousand bottles of Clos de Montmartre every year. To celebrate the grape harvest in early October, the Fêtes des Vendanges (fetesdesvendangesdemontmartre.com), a weeklong festival, is held on the Butte Montmartre and neighbouring districts with wine, food stalls, music and street theatre.

10 Foodie Festivals
Legendary for its cuisine, Paris is a foodie heaven. Try modern cuisine at Omnivore (omnivore.com), a festival in March dedicated to culinary innovation, or savour dishes from leading chefs at Taste of Paris (paris.tastefestivals.com) in May.

A group of cyclists riding past the majestic Arc de Triomphe

TOP 10
SPORTS EVENTS

A marathon in the city centre

1. Paris Marathon
W schneiderelectricparismarathon.com
Runners start at the Champs-Élysées and end at Avenue Foch.

2. Six Nations Rugby
W sixnationsrugby.com
The French team plays England, Scotland, Ireland, Wales and Italy.

3. Ecotrail Paris
W ecotrailparis.com
A trail-running event with courses ranging from beginner- to expert-level.

4. Football Cup Final
W stadefrance.com
The biggest event in French football.

5. French Tennis Open
W rolandgarros.com
This legendary clay-court tournament is part of the prestigious Grand Slam.

6. Top 14 Rugby Final
W stadefrance.com
The world's finest rugby players take part in the French Rugby league finals.

7. Prix de Diane Longines
W francegalop-live.com
An upmarket horse race in Chantilly named after the goddess Diana.

8. La Parisienne
W la-parisienne.net
Europe's largest women-only race in aid of breast cancer research.

9. Qatar Prix de l'Arc de Triomphe
W francegalop-live.com
This world-renowned horse race was first held in 1920.

10. Rolex Paris Masters
W rolexparismasters.com
After the French Open, this is France's next major tennis championship.

AREA BY AREA

A cobbled street by the Seine

ÎLE DE LA CITÉ AND ÎLE ST-LOUIS

Paris was born on the Île de la Cité, an island set on the Seine. It was inhabited by Parisii Gauls around 300 BCE and was then taken over in 52 BCE by Caesar's Romans. Over many centuries, it has been a focus of church and state power and is home to the great cathedral of Notre-Dame and the Palais de Justice. This tiny land mass is also the geographical heart of the city – just outside Notre-Dame is a bronze star embedded in the paving stones with the engraving "Point Zéro", where all distances in Paris are measured from. While the Île de la Cité bustles with tourists, the smaller Île St-Louis, linked to its neighbour by a footbridge, has been an exclusive residential enclave since the 17th century. Its main street is lined with shops, galleries and restaurants and is a lovely place for a stroll

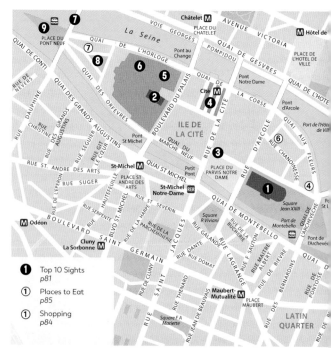

1 Top 10 Sights
p81

1 Places to Eat
p85

1 Shopping
p84

For places to stay in this area, see p176

1 Notre-Dame

This 12th-century Gothic cathedral *(p30)* was listed as a UNESCO World Heritage Site in 1991.

2 Sainte-Chapelle

Known as "a gateway to heaven", this exquisite church *(p44)* was built to house relics collected by St Louis on his crusades.

3 Crypte Archéologique

📍P4 🏛Pl Jean-Paul II, 7500 ⏰10am–6pm Tue–Sun 🌐crypte. paris.fr ♿

Fascinating remnants of early Paris dating back to Gallo-Roman times were discovered in 1965 during an excavation of the square in front of Notre-Dame. The archaeological crypt displays parts of 3rd-century Roman walls, rooms heated by hypocaust, as well as remains of medieval streets and foundations.

Colourful flowers on display at Marché aux Fleurs Reine – Elizabeth II

4 Marché aux Fleurs Reine Elizabeth II

📍N3 🌐marcheauxfleursdeparis.fr

One of the last remaining flower markets in the city centre, the beautiful Marché aux Fleurs *(p72)* is also the oldest, dating from the early 19th century. It is held year-round, Monday to Saturday, in Place Louis-Lépine, filling the north side of the Île de la Cité with dazzling blooms from 8am to 7:30pm. The market was named after Queen Elizabeth II, who visited Paris in 2014 for the 70th anniversary of the D-Day landings.

5 Conciergerie

📍N3 🏛2 Blvd du Palais, 75001 ⏰9:30am–6pm daily 🌐paris-conciergerie.fr ♿

This Gothic palace was built by Philippe le Bel (the Fair) in 1301–15. Parts of it were turned into a prison, controlled by the concierge, or keeper of the king's mansion, hence the name. Ravaillac, assassin of Henri IV, was tortured here, but it was during the Revolution that the prison became a place of terror, when many prisoners were held here awaiting execution by guillotine. Today you can see the Salle des Gardes and the Salle des Gens d'Armes (Hall of the Men-at-Arms), the Bonbec tower and the prison. The cell where Marie-Antoinette was held and the history of other famous Revolution prisoners are on display. Outside, the square Tour de l'Horloge houses the city's first public clock.

0 metres 200
0 yards 200

6 Palais de Justice
🗺 M3 🏛 10 Blvd du Palais, 75001
🕐 9am–6pm Mon–Fri 🌐 cours-appel.
justice.fr

Stretching across the west end of the Île de la Cité, the Palais de Justice, along with the Conciergerie, was once part of the Palais de la Cité, seat of Roman rule and the home of the French kings until 1358. It took its present name during the Revolution – prisoners passed through the Cour du Mai (May Courtyard) on their way to execution during this time – though the Revolutionary Tribunal eventually degenerated during Robespierre's Reign of Terror. In 2018, most of the central law courts that had been housed here moved into new premises in the 17th arrondissement. Make sure to carry your ID for admission.

7 Pont Neuf
🗺 M3

The name – New Bridge – is somewhat incongruous for the oldest surviving bridge in Paris. Following its completion in 1607, Henri IV christened it by charging across on his steed; the bronze equestrian statue of the king was melted down during the Revolution but replaced in 1818. Decorated with striking carved heads, the bridge was unique for its time in that it had no houses built upon it. It has 12 arches and a span of 275 m (912 ft) extending to both sides of the island.

8 Place Dauphine
🗺 M3

In 1607, Henri IV transformed this former royal garden into a triangular square and named it after his son, the Dauphin and future King Louis XIII. Surrounding the square were uniformly built houses of brick and white stone; No 14 is one of the few that retains its original features. One side was destroyed to make way for the expansion of the Palais de Justice. Today this quiet spot is a good place to relax over a drink or meal.

THE GUILLOTINE

Dr Joseph Guillotine invented his "humane" beheading machine at his home near the Odéon, and it was first used in April 1792. During the Revolution some 2,600 prisoners were executed on the Places du Carrousel, de la Concorde, de la Bastille and de la Nation, after awaiting their fate in the Conciergerie prison.

Pont Neuf, Paris's oldest bridge, spanning the Seine

Relaxing at the Square du Vert-Galant on a sunny day

A DAY ON THE ISLANDS

Morning

Admire the exterior of the famous **Notre-Dame** *(p30)*. It is set to reopen in late 2024 after being closed for extensive renovations. From here head for the **Marché aux Fleurs** *(p81)*. You can buy all kinds of garden accessories, flowers and seeds. Take a coffee break at **Le Flore en l'Île** *(p85)*, with its views of the cathedral and the Seine.

Set aside half an hour to visit the **Crypte Archéologique** *(p81)*, before strolling towards **Place Dauphine** *(p82)*. This historic square is a great spot to relax.

There are plenty of places for lunch, but on a sunny day try **La Rose de France** *(p85)*, which has terrace seating.

Afternoon

Soak up the views of the city from **Pont Neuf** *(p82)* before heading towards the **Conciergerie** *(p81)*. See Marie-Antoinette's prison cell in this Gothic palace-turned-prison. Next, spend the rest of the afternoon at the ethereal **Sainte-Chapelle** *(p44)* when the sun beams through the lovely stained-glass windows. From here, start strolling the narrow streets of the **Île St-Louis**, which are filled with shops and galleries *(p84)* offering local products.

Wind up with an afternoon treat by visiting **Berthillon** *(p85)*, considered the best ice cream purveyor in all of France.

9 Square du Vert-Galant
Q M3

Set at the tranquil western tip of the Île de la Cité, this garden is one of the most magical spots in the city. It is accessible from the steps behind Henri IV's statue at Pont Neuf, which bears the nickname of the eccentric monarch, *"vert galant"*, meaning "old flirt". Henry IV did much to beautify Paris in the early 17th century, and his popularity has lasted right up to this day. From here, there is a wonderful view of the Louvre *(p22)* and the Right Bank. It is also the departure point for cruises on the Seine on Les Vedettes du Pont Neuf.

10 Église Saint-Louis-en-l'Île
Q5 **19 Rue St-Louis-en-l'Île, 75004**
7:30am–8pm Mon–Fri, 10am–7:30pm Sat, 8:30am–7pm Sun
saintlouisenlile.catholique.fr

This Baroque church was designed between 1664 and 1726 by the royal architect Louis Le Vau. The exterior features an iron clock (1741) at the entrance and an iron spire, while the interior, richly decorated with gilding and marble, has a statue of St Louis holding his Crusader's sword.

Shopping

1. Lafitte
🚇 P4 🏠 8 Rue Jean du Bellay, 75004
🗓 Sun & Mon

Foie gras and other regional products from the southwest await those looking to indulge in French gastronomy.

2. EFFIGYS
🚇 Q4 🏠 37 Rue Saint-Louis en l'Île, 75004

A souvenir shop aimed at both adults and children, selling Paris-themed gifts, such as hand-cut jigsaw puzzles, perfumed candles and music boxes.

3. Clair de Rêve
🚇 Q5 🏠 35 Rue St-Louis-en-l'Île, 75004 🗓 Sun

This boutique sells original puppets, robots and miniature theatres, making it an ideal shop if you're looking for a present with a difference.

4. Librairie Ulysse
🚇 Q5 🏠 26 Rue St-Louis-en-l'Île, 75004 🗓 Mon–Sun (am only)

Today Paris, tomorrow the world. This eccentric travel bookshop will take you anywhere you want with thousands of titles, antiquarian and new, in French and English – including many on Paris itself.

5. Laguiole
🚇 Q4 🏠 35 Rue des Deux Ponts, 75004 🗓 Sun (am)

Browse an array of knives and cutlery sets from this iconic cutlery brand, which hails from the Aveyron region of southern France. Look for the famous bee motif on the handles.

6. Pylones
🚇 Q5 🏠 57 Rue St-Louis-en-l'Île, 75004 🗓 Thu

Rubber and painted metal are used to create the whimsical jewellery and accessories sold here, along with a selection of novelty gifts.

7. Boulangerie Saint Louis
🚇 Q5 🏠 80 Rue St-Louis -en-l'Île, 75004

One of the few bakeries on the island, this tiny boulangerie has everything classic, ranging from hearty baguette sandwiches to buttery croissants.

8. Maison Moinet
🚇 Q5 🏠 45 Rue St-Louis-en-l'Île, 75004 🗓 Sun & Mon

A family-run confectioner from Vichy, this cute shop sells traditional French sweets and chocolates. It is an enticing treat for all ages.

9. La Ferme Saint-Aubin
🚇 Q5 🏠 76 Rue St-Louis-en-l'Île, 75004 🗓 Mon (am)

Cheese in all shapes and sizes from across France are sold at this *fromagerie*.

10. Carion Minéraux
🚇 Q5 🏠 92 Rue St-Louis-en-l'Île, 75004 🗓 Sun & Mon

There's a wealth of meteorites, fossils and minerals here. Some are made into imaginative jewellery.

Traditional handmade marionette puppets at Clair de Rêve

Places to Eat

Enjoying ice creams and sorbets at Berthillon, a famous ice cream shop

1. Le Saint-Régis

📍 P4 🏠 6 Rue Jean du Bellay, 75004
🌐 lesaintregis-paris.com · €€€

Enjoy classics like duck confit, snails and crème brûlée at this lovely restaurant.

2. Le Sergent Recruteur

📍 Q4 🏠 41 Rue St-Louis-en-l'Île, 75004
🕐 L Sun, Mon & Tue 🌐 lesergent recruteur.fr · €€€

Served in a stylishly refurbished space, the Michelin-starred tasting menus include imaginative modern interpretations of traditional dishes.

3. Les Fous de L'Île

📍 Q4 🏠 33 Rue des Deux Ponts, 75004
🌐 lesfous.paris · €€

This modern Parisian bistro serves typical dishes such as *entrecôte* or steak tartare. It also hosts exhibitions and live music.

4. Le Petit Plateau

📍 G5 🏠 1 Quai aux Fleurs, 75004
🌐 le-petit-plateau-restaurant-paris. eatbu.com · €

This tearoom is a great lunch spot, serving delicious home-made salads, quiches and cakes.

5. Brasserie de l'Îsle St-Louis

📍 P4 🏠 55 Quai de Bourbon, 75004
🕐 Wed, Aug 🌐 labrasserie-isl.fr · €€

Wooden tables and a rustic look complement hearty Alsace fare,

such as tripe in Riesling wine. The terrace welcomes alfresco diners in summer.

6. Au Vieux Paris d'Arcole

📍 N4 🏠 24 Rue Chanoinesse, 75004
🌐 restaurantauvieuxparis.fr · €€€

This charming restaurant, with its wisteria-clad façade, is set in one of the oldest buildings on the Île de la Cité, dating from 1512. The menu features hearty Auvergnat cuisine.

7. La Rose de France

📍 M3 🏠 24 Pl Dauphine, 75001
🌐 larosedefrance.fr · €€

Dine on French classics on the lovely terrace or in the cosy dining room.

8. L'Îlot Vache

📍 Q5 🏠 35 Rue St Louis en l'Île, 75004 🌐 lilotvache.fr · €€

French classics still have some surprises – duck confit with rasp-berries, for example – at this tiny, unpretentious restaurant. The table displays of flowers are spectacular.

9. Le Flore en l'Île

📍 P5 🏠 42 Quai d'Orléans, 75004
🌐 lefloreenlile.fr · €€

Go for the views as well as the food at this bistro-cum-tearoom, open from breakfast until 2am.

10. Berthillon

📍 G5 🏠 31 Rue St-Louis-en-l'Île, 75004 🕐 Mon & Tue 🌐 berthillon.fr · €

There is always a queue outside this legendary ice cream and sorbet shop and tearoom but it is worth the wait.

BEAUBOURG AND LES HALLES

The small but lively Beaubourg Quarter, brimming with art galleries and cafés, has become a major tourist attraction since the Centre Georges Pompidou opened in 1977. Neighbouring Les Halles, meanwhile, was once home to the city's main food market, and today remains a big destination for food lovers, thanks to its excellent bistros, speciality food shops and buzzing bars.

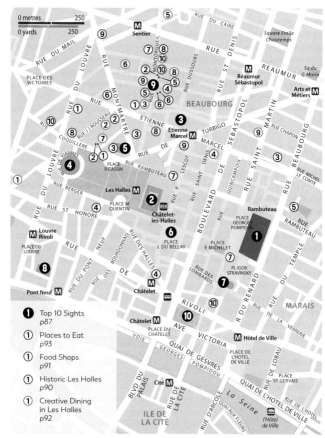

1	Top 10 Sights	p87
1	Places to Eat	p93
1	Food Shops	p91
1	Historic Les Halles	p90
1	Creative Dining in Les Halles	p92

For places to stay in this area, see p176

1 Centre Georges Pompidou

P2 Pl Georges Pompidou, 75004 For renovation centre pompidou.fr

This cross-cultural arts complex was built by architects Richard Rogers and Renzo Piano, who turned the building "inside-out" to show brightly coloured utility pipes on the façade. It houses the Musée National d'Art Moderne, as well as a library, shops, two cinemas and a performance space. It is closed for renovation work, with exhibits loaned to the Louvre (p22), Musée d'Orsay (p26) and Grand Palais (p113).

2 Westfield Forum des Halles

N2 westfield.com/en/france/ forumdeshalles

This underground shopping mall contains an array of shops, including a FNAC bookshop, alongside restaurants, cinemas, a conservatoire and a centre for hip-hop (La Place), the first of its kind in France. The complex is topped by a huge undulating glass-and-steel roof, dubbed "the Canopy", and the surrounding gardens are beautifully landscaped.

3 Tour Jean Sans Peur

N1 20 Rue Etienne Marcel, 75002 1:30–6pm Wed–Sun tour jeansanspeur.wordpress.com

After the Duke of Orléans was assassin-ated on his orders in 1407, the Duke of Burgundy feared reprisals. To protect himself, he built this 27-m- (88-ft-) tall tower onto his home, the Hôtel de Bourgogne, and moved his bedroom up to the fourth floor. A remnant of the 15th-century residence, the tower later became a theatre in the 17th to 18th centuries. Today it hosts exhibitions on life in the Middle Ages.

4 Bourse de Commerce – Collection Pinault

M1 2 Rue de Viarmes, 75001 11am–7pm Wed–Mon (to 9pm Fri) pinaultcollection.com

A former grain market and then Commodities Exchange, this

The richly decorated dome of Bourse de Commerce – Collection Pinault

impressive circular building, dating from 1767, has been transformed into an exhibition space housing the substantial collection of billionaire businessman François Pinault's contemporary art. As well as an array of changing art exhibitions, there are music concerts, film screenings and conferences.

5 Église St-Eustache

M1 2 Impasse St-Eustache, 75001 10am–6pm Mon–Fri, 10am–7pm Sat & Sun saint-eustache.org

With its majestic arches and pillars, Église St-Eustache is one of the most beautiful churches in Paris. Although Gothic in design, it took 105 years to build (1532–1637) and its interior decoration reflects the Renaissance style of this time. The church was modelled on Notre-Dame (p30), with double side aisles and a ring of side chapels. The stained-glass windows made from sketches by Philippe de Champaigne (1631) and the tomb of politician Jean-Baptiste Colbert (1619–83) are the highlights.

6 Fontaine des Innocents

N2 Rue St-Denis & Rue Berger, 75001

Place Joachim-du-Bellay is a pretty tree-lined square in Les Halles. It was built atop a cemetery in the 18th century, from which the remains of some two million people were transferred to the Catacombs (p62) at Denfert-Rochereau. The square's highlight is the Renaissance Fontaine des Innocents, the last of its era built in the city, which was designed by Pierre Lescot and carved by sculptor Jean Goujon in 1547. The fountain originally stood against a wall on Rue St-Denis, and was moved to the new square, when a fourth side was added.

7 Église St-Merry

P2 76 Rue de la Verrerie, 75004 8am–8pm Mon–Sat, 9am–1pm & 3:30–6pm Sun paroissesaintmerry.fr

Formerly the parish church of the Lombard moneylenders, St-Merry was built between 1520 and 1612, and reflects the Flamboyant Gothic style. Its name is a corruption of St Médéric, who was buried on this site in the early 8th century. The bell in the church's northwest turret, thought to be the oldest in Paris, dates from 1331. Other highlights include the decorative west front, the 17th-century organ loft, beautiful stained glass and carved wood panelling. There are free concerts at the weekends.

8 St-Germain l'Auxerrois

M2 2 Pl du Louvre, 75001 9am–7pm daily saintgermain auxerrois.fr

When the Valois kings moved to the Louvre palace (p22) in the 14th century, this became the church of the royal family. On 24 August 1572, the tolling of its bell was used as the signal for the St Bartholomew's Day Massacre, when thousands of Huguenots who had come to Paris for the wedding of Henri of Navarre to Marguerite of Valois (p32) were murdered. The church features a range of architectural styles, from its Flamboyant Gothic façade to its Renaissance choir. Check the website for details about the monthly guided tours.

GEORGES POMPIDOU

Georges Pompidou (1911–74) had the unenviable task of following Charles de Gaulle as president of France, from 1969 until his death. During his tenure, he initiated many architectural developments in Paris, including the controversial but ultimately successful Pompidou Centre, and the less popular scheme to demolish Les Halles market.

Enjoying a drink at Café Montorgueil on Rue Montorgueil

9 Rue Montorgueil

N1 rue-montorgueil.com

This bustling market street was once part of the oldest marketplace in Paris, the historic Les Halles. Today, the picturesque street has countless wine shops, bistros, boutiques, restaurants and gourmet cheese and pastry shops, all of which are a visitor's delight. Many Parisian chefs frequent the shops along Rue Montorgueil, along with locals and tourists alike. Its charming and lively cafés are perfect for people-watching after indulging in delicious treats from any of its excellent bakeries.

10 Tour St-Jacques

N3 Sq de la Tour St-Jacques, 75004 boutique. toursaintjacques.fr

The late Gothic tower, dating from 1523, is all that remains of the church of St-Jacques-la-Boucherie, once the largest medieval church in Paris and a starting point for pilgrims on their journey to Santiago de Compostela in Spain. In the 17th century the mathematician and physicist Blaise Pascal used the tower for barometrical experiments. The church was pulled down after the Revolution. Visitors can take a tour to the top of the tower and visit the gardens (book online).

Stained-glass window showing St Anthony of Padua at the Église St-Merry

A DAY IN LES HALLES

Morning

Start your day with coffee and a hearty breakfast at Copains (*60 Rue Tiquetonne*), a gluten-free and vegan bakery. Once you're done, head to the **Bourse de Commerce – Collection Pinault** (*p87*) to explore its modern art collection; the elaborately painted ceilings here are a sight to behold.

Afterwards, take a short stroll to Place Igor Stravinsky and admire the colourful **Stravinsky Fountain** (*p61*).

Having booked ahead, take your seat at Michelin-starred bistro **Benoit** (*p93*), whose lunchtime menu is far cheaper than in the evening.

Afternoon

Pass the **Fontaine des Innocents** as you head for Les Halles, but first pay a visit to the **Église St-Eustache** (*p87*), where the workers of the old Les Halles market worshipped.

Walk under the green canopy over the **Westfield Forum des Halles** (*p87*) and head for charming **Rue Montorgueil** and the little streets surrounding it – there are plenty of food shops and cafés to explore.

Finish the day at the classic brasserie **Au Pied de Cochon** (*p93*), a great spot for comfort foods such as pork terrine and onion soup *au gratin*.

Hand-painted murals in the Parisian brasserie Au Pied de Cochon

Historic Les Halles

1. Au Pied de Cochon
This 24-hour brasserie (*p93*) still serves dishes that used to appeal to the earthy tastes of market workers, including the eponymous pigs' trotters.

2. Le Cochon à l'Oreille
F3 15 Rue Montmartre, 75001
Dating back to the early 20th century, this ornate former working men's café/bar, decorated with historic tiles and murals, has only a small dining room, so book in advance.

3. Église St-Eustache Sculpture
The sculpture by Raymond Mason in the church's (*p87*) Chapelle des Pélerins d'Emmaüs is a tribute to the beloved market. Its colourful figures depict *The Departure of Fruit and Vegetables from the Heart of Paris, 28 February 1969*.

4. Aurouze
F4 8 Rue des Halles, 75001
This shop is credited with getting rid of Les Halles' most unwelcome inhabitants – rats. The window display is a taxidermy tribute to the once-common vermin.

5. Stöhrer
N1 51 Rue Montorgueil, 75002
Stöhrer is one of Paris's loveliest old-fashioned patisseries, founded in 1730 by a chef who had worked for Louis XV.

6. Au Rocher de Cancale
N1 78 Rue Montorgueil, 75002
Once a gathering space for artists and writers during the early 19th century, this place is known for its oysters.

7. La Fresque
N1 100 Rue Rambuteau, 75001
This wonderful restaurant used to be a fishmonger. Original tiles and a fresco of a fishing scene still decorate the back room.

8. E. Dehillerin
M1 18 Rue Coquillière, 75001
Since 1820, everyone from army cooks to gourmet chefs has come here for copper pots, cast-iron pans and cooking utensils.

9. Duthilleul et Minart
P1 14 Rue de Turbigo, 75001
For more than 100 years this shop has sold French work clothes and uniforms, such as chefs' hats and watchmakers' smocks.

10. À la Cloche des Halles
M1 28 Rue Coquillière, 75001
This wine bar and restaurant practically chimes with history. The "cloche" is the bronze bell whose peal once signalled the start and end of the market day.

Food Shops

1. G. Detou
N1 58 Rue Tiquetonne, 75002
The shelves at this chef's paradise are laden with chocolates, teas, artisanal mustards and more.

2. Mariage Frères
N1 90 Rue Montorgueil, 75002
This elegant and fragrant tea boutique has a dizzying array of teas and teapots.

3. Charles Chocolatier
N1 15 Rue Montorgueil, 75002
On a cold day, stop in at this family-run chocolate shop for a take-away cup of their luscious hot chocolate; the ice creams in summer are delectable, too.

4. À la Mère de Famille
N1 82 Rue Montorgueil, 75002
This branch of the oldest confectionary shop in Paris stocks regional French sweets, all in the brand's vintage-inspired packaging.

5. La Fermette
N1 86 Rue Montorgueil, 75002
The enthusiastic cheesemongers here are ready with tips and tastings to help visitors make the perfect choice from the piles of cheese on display.

Assortments of chocolates at the À la Mère de Famille

Browsing the baked treats on display at Maison Collet boulangerie

6. Boucherie Roger
N1 62 Rue Montorgueil, 75002
From tender roasted chicken to meat pâté, this place has it all. They even offers delicious cuts prepared in-house.

7. Delitaly
F3 5 Rue des Petits Carreaux, 75002
You'll find fresh and dried pastas, gourmet olive oils, tubs of antipasti and a mouthwatering selection of salami and other cured meats at this Italian deli.

8. Eric Kayser
F3 16 Rue des Petits Carreaux, 75002
Beyond excellent baguettes, choose from all manner of delicious pastries and other baked goods to stock up on for tea.

9. Librairie Gourmande
F3 92–96 Rue Montmartre, 75002
This fabulous bookshop has an extensive collection of books on wine and cooking, some in English.

10. Maison Collet
N1 100 Rue Montorgueil, 75002
Run by the same family for two generations, this boulangerie is known for its viennoiseries and light-as-air meringues.

Creative Dining in Les Halles

High wooden chairs at Pitanga, a tapas bar

1. Pitanga
⚑ M1 ⌖ 11 Rue Jean-Jacques Rousseau, 75001 ☏ 01 40 28 12 69
Brazilian-born gastro chef Alexandre Furtado's tapas bar serves up delicious modern French-Latin American cuisine.

2. Ô Château
⚑ M1 ⌖ 68 Rue J J Rousseau, 75001
Get tips for buying wine at Ô Château. This wine bar runs very popular sessions with English-speaking sommeliers. Consider a tasting dinner in one of their vaulted cellars.

3. Fou de Patisserie
⚑ N1 ⌖ 45 Rue Montorgueil, 75002
This retailer excels in bringing the best pastries from around the city to Les Halles. Sample pastries from some of Paris's most popular chefs such as Pierre Hermé and Cyril Lignac. Here, shoppers can find cakes and other creative products by Paris's biggest names.

4. TranTranZai
⚑ N1 ⌖ 94 Rue Saint-Denis
ⓦ trantranzai.fr
The speciality at this popular Sichuan restaurant is its handpulled Dan Dan noodles. Other favourites include the homemade dumplings and flavourful pepper-packed soup broths.

5. Boneshaker Donuts
⚑ F3 ⌖ 86 Rue d'Abouhir, 75002
Away from the traditional pastry shops of Les Halles, Boneshaker produces delicious gourmet, small batch doughnuts.

6. La Cevicheria
⚑ F3 ⌖ 14 Rue Bachaumont, 75002
Try some fresh ceviche – a speciality of raw fish from various Latin American countries. At La Cevicheria it is inspired by the Peruvian version.

7. Lai'Tcha
⚑ M1 ⌖ 7 Rue du Jour, 75002
Michelin-starred chef Adeline Grattard's casual eatery, housed in a handsome modern space, is a dumpling bar in the daytime and a Chinese bistro in the evening – think scallop sticky rice and king crab rolls.

8. Experimental Cocktail Club
⚑ F3 ⌖ 37 Rue St Sauveur, 75002
Although French wine will always reign supreme, the cocktails at this speakeasy-style bar are a welcome addition to the drink options in Les Halles. Dress to impress and prepare to elbow your way to the busy bar.

9. Qasti
⚑ G3 ⌖ 205 Rue Saint Martin, 75003
ⓦ qasti.fr
Run by Michelin-starred chef Alan Geeam, Qasti is a popular Lebanese restaurant. Choose from mezzes or dishes such as cod in tahini sauce.

10. Grillé
⚑ N1 ⌖ 6 Rue des Petits Carreaux, 75002
A new-generation gourmet kebab spot, Grillé serves high-quality meats and baked-to-order flatbreads.

Places to Eat

1. Kitchen by Stéphanie Le Quellec
🗺 M1 🏠 48 Rue du Louvre, 75001
🌐 madamereve.com · €€€
Try classics like steak tartare, foie gras and chocolate mousse by one of France's top chefs at this grand café.

2. Au Pied de Cochon
🗺 M1 🏠 6 Rue Coquillière, 75001
🌐 pieddecochon.com · €€
A Les Halles favourite, Au Pied de Cochon specializes in pork dishes. There are traditional brasserie options too, such as oysters and steak.

3. L'Ambassade d'Auvergne
🗺 P1 🏠 22 Rue du Grenier St-Lazare, 75003 🕐 Two weeks in Aug
🌐 ambassade-auvergne.fr · €€
With the ambience of a rustic inn, this restaurant transports you to rural Auvergne. Plenty of pork and cabbage dishes, as well as sausage and aligot, are served here.

4. Tour de Montlhéry, Chez Denise
🗺 M2 🏠 5 Rue des Prouvaires, 75001
☎ 01 42 36 21 82 🕐 Mid-Jul–mid-Aug: Sat & Sun · €€
A Les Halles legend for its huge portions and convivial atmosphere. Book in advance.

5. Le Hangar
🗺 G4 🏠 12 Impasse Berthaud, 75003
☎ 01 42 74 55 44 🕐 Sun & Mon · €€
This small, friendly bistro is no secret to the locals, who keep returning for the fabulous food, including the steak tartare and great desserts such as moelleux au chocolat.

6. Le Tambour
🗺 N1 🏠 41 Rue Montmartre, 75002
🌐 menuonline.fr/letambour/carte-restaurant · €€
This bistro draws a lively crowd with its friendly service and hearty French fare.

PRICE CATEGORIES
For a three-course meal for one with half a bottle of wine (or equivalent meal), taxes and extra charges
....
€ under €30 €€ €30–€50 €€€ over €50

7. Café Beaubourg
🗺 P2 🏠 43 Rue St-Merri, 75001
🌐 cafebeaubourg.com · €€€
The terrace here overlooks the Pompidou Centre. Steak tartare is a house special.

8. L'Escargot Montorgueil
🗺 N1 🏠 38 Rue Montorgueil, 75001
🌐 escargotmontorgueil.com · €€€
At the heart of Rue Montorgueil, this Parisian institution is known for its signature French dish of snails, after which it is named. Enjoy the view from the terrace.

9. Aux Crues de Bourgogne
🗺 N1 🏠 3 Rue Bachaumont, 75002
🌐 auxcrusdebourgogne.com · €€€
A classic French bistro with menu items that include boeuf bourguignon, vol-au-vent and steak au poivre.

10. Benoît
🗺 P1 🏠 20 Rue St-Martin, 75004
🕐 Aug 🌐 benoit-paris.com · €€€
Opened in 1912, this Michelin-starred location is, justifiably, the most expensive bistro in Paris. Try the lunchtime menu to keep the cost down.

The elegant interior of Michelin-starred Benoît

MARAIS AND THE BASTILLE

For many, the Marais is one of the most enjoyable quarters of Paris, thanks to its chic shops, cutting-edge galleries and bustling restaurants. It is also home to countless Renaissance mansions, many of which house excellent museums, such as the Musée Carnavalet and Musée Cognacq-Jay. East of this area sits the Bastille, historically infamous as the birthplace of the Revolution. Today, though, visitors are drawn here by its creative ateliers, independent boutiques and lively nightlife.

For places to stay in this area, see p176

A 17th-century arcade in Place des Vosges with antique shops

1 Place des Vosges

Ⓜ R3

Paris's oldest square – one of the world's most beautiful – was commissioned by Henri IV in 1605. Its 36 houses with red-gold brick and stone façades, slate roofs and dormer windows were laid out with striking symmetry in 1612. While the buildings were originally meant to house silk weavers, the likes of Cardinal Richelieu (1585–1642) and playwright Molière (1622–73) quickly moved in. However, everyone can enjoy a stroll around the area and visit the art galleries under the arcades.

2 Musée Cognacq-Jay

Ⓜ Q3 🏛 8 Rue Elzévir, 75003 ◷ 10am–6pm Tue–Sun 🖥 musee cognacqjay.paris.fr

This small but excellent museum illustrates French lifestyle in the so-called Age of Enlightenment, which centred on Paris. The beautiful 18th-century art and furniture on display were once the private collection of Ernest Cognacq and his wife, Marie-Louise Jay, founders of the former Samaritaine department store by Pont Neuf. It is superbly displayed in the Hôtel Donon, an elegant late-16th-century mansion.

3 Musée Picasso

After Pablo Picasso died in 1973, his family donated thousands of his works to the French state in lieu of estate taxes. Thus Paris has the largest collection of Picassos in the world. Housed in the Hôtel Salé, which was extensively renovated in late 2014, the collection (p40) displays the range of his artistic development and reveals his mastery in a wide range of techniques and materials. Larger sculptures are housed in the garden and courtyard of the museum. Entry is free on the first Sunday of every month.

The Colonne de Juillet towering over Place de la Bastille

4 Opéra National de Paris Bastille

H5 **Pl de la Bastille, 75012** **operadeparis.fr**

Designed by architect Carlos Ott and constructed from steel, glass and concrete, this modern opera theatre is the largest in Paris, with a 2,745-seat auditorium. Tours of the building provide access to backstage areas.

5 Musée Carnavalet

R3 **23 Rue de Sévigné Bourgeois, 75003** **10am–6pm Tue–Sun** **carnavalet.paris.fr**

Devoted to the history of Paris, this fascinating museum sprawls through two mansions, the 16th-century Carnavalet and 17th-century Le Peletier de Saint-Fargeau. The former was the home of Madame de Sévigné, the famous letter-writer, from 1677 to 1696 and a gallery here is devoted to her life. The extensive museum contains period rooms filled with art and portraits, plus Revolutionary artifacts and memorabilia of 18th-century philosophers Rousseau and Voltaire.

6 Place de la Bastille

H5

Originally, the Bastille was a fortress built by Charles V to defend the eastern edge of the city, but it soon became a jail for political prisoners. Angry citizens, rising up against the excesses of the monarchy, stormed the Bastille on 14 July 1789 (*p9*) and destroyed this hated symbol of oppression, sparking the French Revolution. In its place is the bronze 52-m- (171-ft-) high Colonne de Juillet (July Column), crowned by the Angel of Liberty, which commemorates those who died in the 1830 and 1848 revolutions. Behind it is the Opéra Bastille, once the largest opera house in the world, which opened on the bicentennial of the Revolution in 1989. In order to divert traffic, certain sections of this busy square have now been pedestrianized.

7 The Passages

H5

The Bastille has been the quarter of working-class artisans and craft guilds since the 17th century and many furniture makers are still located in these small alleyways, called *passages*. Rue du Faubourg St-Antoine is lined with shops selling a striking array of traditional period furniture and modern designs, but don't miss the narrow *passages*, such as Passage L'Homme, that run off this and other streets in the Bastille.

THE JEWISH QUARTER

The Jewish Quarter, centred on rues des Rosiers and des Écouffes, was established in the 13th century and has attracted immigrants since the Revolution. Many Jews fled here to escape persecution in Eastern Europe, but were arrested during the Nazi Occupation. Since World War II, Sephardic Jews from North Africa have found new homes here.

Many artists and craftspeople have their ateliers (workshops) in these atmospheric alleys.

8 Musée de la Chasse et de la Nature

☐ Q2 ☐ 62 Rue des Archives, 75003 ☐ 11am–6pm Tue–Sun (to 9:30pm Wed, except Jul & Aug) ☐ Public hols ☐ chassenature.org ☐

Occupying two well-preserved 17th- and 18th-century mansions, this refurbished museum explores the history of hunting, and humanity's relationship with the natural world. Curated to resemble the home of a rich collector, the museum displays tapestries and gilt-framed period paintings alongside taxidermy animals and fascinating curiosity cabinets. There are surprises in each elegantly organized room, from the astonishing Jan Fabre-designed ceiling of owl feathers to the sleepy fox curled up on a chair.

9 Maison Européenne de la Photographie

☐ Q3 ☐ 5–7 Rue de Fourcy, 75004 ☐ 11am–8pm Wed–Fri, 10am–8pm Sat & Sun ☐ mep-fr.org ☐

This excellent gallery showcases contemporary European photography. It is housed in an early-18th century mansion, Hôtel Hénault de Cantorbre, where a mix of historic features and modern spaces shows off the gallery's permanent collection and changing exhibitions of items from its archives.

10 Maison de Victor Hugo

☐ R4 ☐ 6 Pl des Vosges, 75004 ☐ 10am–6pm Tue–Sun ☐ Public hols ☐ maisonsvictorhugo.paris.fr ☐

French author Victor Hugo (1802–85) lived on the second floor of the Hôtel de Rohan-Guémenée, the largest house on the Place des Vosges, from 1832 to 1848. He wrote most of *Les Misérables* here, among other works. In 1903, the house became a museum covering his life. There is no entry fee for the apartment.

A DAY IN THE MARAIS

Morning

Begin at the **Musée Carnavalet** and immerse yourself in the history of Paris. Later, walk to the **Place des Vosges** (p95): take in the whole square from the fountains in the centre.

Have a coffee at **Ma Bourgogne** (19 Pl des Vosges), right on the square. Head towards **Maison de Victor Hugo**, then go to the south-west corner of the square, through a wooden door to the garden of the **Hôtel de Béthune-Sully** (p98).

Afternoon

If the weather is nice, join the queue at **L'As du Fallafel** (p103) for a falafel wrap to eat in nearby square Charles-Victor Langlois. Otherwise, head for the **Marché des Enfants Rouges** (p103) and its international food stalls.

Spend the afternoon exploring the Marais and its shops and cafés. Pop into the fashionable boutiques along the **Rue des Francs Bourgeois** and **Rue Vieille du Temple**; have a slice of babka in the Jewish Quarter on **Rue des Rosiers**; then explore the Upper Marais, where concept store **Merci** (p100) holds court.

Walk through **Place de la Bastille** – once the city's dreaded prison – on the way to enjoy dinner beneath the chandeliers of **Le Train Bleu** (20 Blvd Diderot), set inside the Gare de Lyon train station.

Mansions

1. Hôtel de Soubise
🅚 Q2 🅐 60 Rue des Francs Bourgeois, 75003 🕐 10am–5:30pm Mon, Wed–Fri, 2–5:30pm Sat & Sun

Along with the adjacent Hôtel de Rohan, this mansion contains the national archives.

2. Hôtel Salé
Built in 1656–9 for Aubert de Fontenay, a salt-tax collector, this mansion is now the home of the Musée Picasso (p40).

3. Hôtel Guénégaud
🅚 P3 🅐 60 Rue des Archives, 75003 🗗

Designed by the architect François Mansart in the mid-17th century, this splendid mansion houses the Musée de la Chasse et de la Nature (p97).

4. Hôtel de Beauvais
🅚 P3 🅐 68 Rue François Miron, 75004 🗗 To the public

The young Mozart performed at this 17th-century mansion. Notice the balcony decorated with goats' heads.

5. Hôtel de St-Aignan
🅚 P2 🅐 71 Rue du Temple, 75003 🕐 11am–6pm Tue–Fri, 10am–7pm Sat & Sun (for permanent exhibits) 🆆 mahj.org 🗗

This enormous mansion is now the Museum of Jewish Art and History.

6. Hôtel de Coulanges
🅚 Q2 🅐 35 Rue des Francs Bourgeois, 75004

This 17th-century mansion is now a concept store and cultural space.

7. Hôtel de Béthune-Sully
🅚 R4 🅐 62 Rue St-Antoine, 7500 🗗 To the public, except the bookshop 🆆 hotel-de-sully.fr

Headquarters of the Centre des Monuments Nationaux, the Hôtel de Béthune-Sully has a bookshop on French culture and heritage.

8. Hôtel de Lamoignon
🅚 Q3 🅐 24 Rue Pavée, 75004 🕐 10am–6pm Mon–Sat

This mansion houses the Bibliothèque Historique de la Ville de Paris.

9. Hôtel de Marle
🅚 G4 🅐 11 Rue Payenne, 75003 🕐 Noon–6pm Wed–Sun; café: noon–6pm Tue–Sun

The Swedish Institute and its pretty courtyard café are located here.

10. Hôtel de Sens
🅚 Q4 🅐 7 Rue des Nonnains d'Hyères, 75004 🗗 To the public, except the library

Henri IV's wife Marguerite de Valois lived here after their divorce. It now houses a fine arts library.

Inside the historic Hôtel Salé, home to the Musée Picasso

Galleries

The exterior of the excellent Galerie Marian Goodman

1. Galerie Marian Goodman
P2 **79 Rue du Temple, 75003** **Noon–6pm Tue–Sat** **mariangoodman.com**
Housed in a 17th-century mansion, this gallery is a slice of New York style. Artists include Jeff Wall and video-maker Steve McQueen.

2. Galerie Akié Arichi
H5 **26 Rue Keller, 75011** **2–7pm Tue–Sat** **ahiearichi.com**
Exhibitions here cover photography, sculpture and painting, often with an Asian influence.

3. Galerie Alain Gutharc
H4 **7 Rue St-Claude, 75003** **11am–7pm Tue–Sat** **alaingutharc.com**
Alain Gutharc devotes this space to the work of contemporary French artists.

4. Templon Paris
P2 **30 Rue Beaubourg, 75003** **10am–7pm Tue–Sat** **Aug** **templon.com**
A favourite among the French contemporary art establishment, this gallery exhibits cutting-edge artists.

5. Galerie Karsten Greve
R2 **5 Rue Debelleyme, 75003** **10am–7pm Tue–Sat** **galerie-karsten-greve.com**
A leading international gallery with top names in modern and contemporary art and photography.

6. Galerie Patrick Seguin
H4 **5 Rue des Taillandiers, 75011** **10am–7pm Mon–Sat** **patrickseguin.com**
This gallery features stylish 20th-century furniture and architecture, including works by French architect and designer Jean Prouvé.

7. Galerie Thaddeus Ropac
Q1 **7 Rue Debelleyme, 75003** **10am–7pm Tue–Sat** **ropac.net**
A major contemporary gallery, Thaddeus Ropac exhibits new and influential international artists.

8. Galeries Nathalie Obadia
P2 **3 Rue du Cloître Saint-Merri, 75004** **11am–7pm Mon–Sat** **nathalieobadia.com**
This space exhibits a wide range of contemporary art from both French and international artists.

9. Perrotin Paris
R2 **76 Rue de Turenne, 75003** **10am–6pm Tue–Sat** **perrotin.com**
One of the most prestigious art galleries in Paris, Perrotin hosts some of the world's leading contemporary artists such as Takashi Murakami and Mathilde Denize.

10. Galerie20Vosges
H4 **20 Pl des Vosges 75004** **11am–7:30pm Wed–Sun** **galerie20vosges.com**
Contemporary artists, painters and sculptors showcase their unique work under the arcades of the regal Place des Vosges.

Fashion and Accessory Shops

A variety of products at the popular concept store, Merci

1. Merci
Q R2 **A** 111 Blvd Beaumarchais, 75003
This trendy multi-brand store stocks clothes and accessories alongside stylish homewares.

2. Anatomica
Q P3 **A** 14 Rue du Bourg Tibourg, 75004
If you are looking for a place to buy men's clothing, don't give this a miss. One of the city's best men's stores, it carries perfectly tailored clothes and leather shoes from cult brand Alden.

3. Eric Bompard
Q R3 **A** 14 Rue de Sévigné, 75004
Everything is soft at this cashmere specialist – jumpers, scarves, gloves and much more.

4. Antoine et Lili
Q Q2 **A** 51 Rue des Francs Bourgeois, 75004
Behind the bright pink shopfront, chic clothes for women are inspired by Romani and Asian styles, and made using vibrant natural fabrics. It also sells children's clothes and home furnishings.

5. Bensimon-Home Autour du Monde
Q G4 **A** 8 Rue des Francs Bourgeois, 75003 **W** bensimon.com
French designer Serge Bensimon's popular concept store stocks the brand's classic canvas sneakers in bright colours, limited-edition patterns and pretty Liberty prints for kids as well as adults.

6. Monsieur Paris
Q R1 **A** 53 Rue Charlot, 75003
This store sells delicate gold and silver jewellery. Designer Nadia Azoug is often at work in the on-site atelier.

7. Sessùn
Q H5 **A** 34 Rue de Charonne, 75011
This is the flagship store of the young, French womenswear label, which has chic, edgy clothes and accessories.

8. K. Jacques
Q Q3 **A** 16 Rue Pavée, 75004
The classic Saint-Tropez sandal, given iconic status by Brigitte Bardot, is stocked here, in some 60 styles and colours.

9. Isabel Marant
Q H5 **A** 16 Rue de Charonne, 75011
This designer is getting a lot of recognition outside France for her hip but elegant pieces.

10. Bonton
Q R1 **A** 5 Blvd des Filles du Calvaire, 75003
A gorgeous store for kids, Bonton has three levels of clothes, accessories, toys and even a vintage photo booth.

Specialist Shops

1. Mariage Frères
Q3 **30 Rue du Bourg Tibourg, 75004**
This famous tea house was founded in 1854 and sells all kinds of blends, as well as tea-making paraphernalia.

2. Jacques Genin
G3 **133 Rue de Turenne, 75003**
This trendy chocolatier is adored for his caramels and fruit jellies. He also bakes a fantastic millefeuille.

3. La Manufacture de Chocolat
H4 **40 Rue de la Roquette, 75011**
The *chocolaterie* of Michelin-starred chef Alain Ducasse smells divine – and has the taste to back it up.

4. Fragonard
Q2 **51 Rue des Francs Bourgeois, 75004**
If you can't visit this perfume-maker's factory in the south of France, pick up some soaps and scents in this fragrant boutique.

5. CSAO
G4 **9 Rue Elzévir, 75003**
The Compagnie du Sénégal et de l'Afrique de l'Ouest sells a bright and colourful array of homewares such as woven bags, hand-painted plates and embroidered cushions.

6. L'Arbre à Lettres
H5 **62 Rue du Faubourg St-Antoine, 75012**
This beautiful bookshop specializes in fine arts, literature and social sciences.

7. Liquides Bar à Parfum
G3 **9 Rue Normandie, 75003**
Behind its elegant black storefront in the Upper Marais, Liquides carries scents that you won't find anywhere else.

8. Papier Tigre
R1 **5 Rue des Filles du Calvaire, 75003**
Stylish graphic notebooks, greeting cards and other quirkily designed paper products are on offer at this modern stationery shop.

9. Izraël
P3 **30 Rue François Miron, 75004**
Also called the "World of Spices", this tiny store is a treasure trove of cheese, wine, rum, honey, mustard and myriad other delights.

10. Village Saint Paul
R4 **Between Rue St-Paul and Rue des Jardins St-Paul, 75004**
An intriguing maze of art galleries, fine antiques and design shops, tucked away behind Église St-Paul.

Chocolate genius Jacques Genin's exquisite millefeuille

Fashionable Hangouts

Outdoor tables at Le Progrès, a typical Parisian bar

1. Andy Wahloo
Q1 ◫ 69 Rue des Gravilliers, 75003
In one of Henri IV's former mansions, pop art and North African decor form a backdrop for fashionable soirées.

2. Zéro Zéro
H4 ◫ 89 Rue Amelot, 75011
It doesn't get much cooler than this den-like bar with wood panelling and flowered wallpaper. Though not listed on the menu, cocktails are a speciality.

3. La Perle
Q2 ◫ 78 Rue Vieille du Temple, 75003 ⓦ cafelaperle.com
This is one of Paris's most famous hangouts. Its straightforward menu draws a fashionable crowd in the evenings.

4. La Caféothèque de Paris
P4 ◫ 52 Rue de l'Hôtel de Ville, 75004
Coffee enthusiasts congregate at this cool coffee roaster located behind the Hôtel de Ville for some excellent brews.

It also has a shop that stocks coffee beans and unusual jams, as well as a coffee-tasting school.

5. La Mezcaleria Paris
R1 ◫ 13 Blvd du Temple, 75003
Hidden behind the kitchen at the Hotel 1K, this Mexican-themed speakeasy serves creative cocktails, Mezcal, tequila and tacos in a colourful space.

6. Café de l'Industrie
H4 ◫ 16 Rue St-Sabin, 75011
This is a fashionable and sizable café that has three rooms where the walls are lined with paintings and old-fashioned artifacts. The food is inexpensive but pretty good, and the later it gets the better the buzz.

7. Grazie
H4 ◫ 91 Blvd Beaumarchais, 75003
ⓦ graziegrazie.fr
An Italian pizzeria with an industrial loft-style decor, Grazie serves authentic pizzas and classy cocktails, and attracts a hip crowd.

8. Le Panic Room
H4 ◫ 101 Rue Amelot, 75011
Top Parisian DJs set the tone at this quirky bar offering fancy cocktails, a smoking room and cellar dance floor.

9. Le Square Trousseau
H5 ◫ 1 Rue Antoine Vollon, 75012
This charming Bastille district brasserie, with its lovely heated terrace, is something of a media haunt, serving good food from breakfast into the early hours.

10. Le Progrès
R2 ◫ 1 Rue de Bretagne, 75003
ⓦ leprogresmarais.fr
The terrace of this corner café in the trendy Upper Marais is the place to be during Paris Fashion Week.

Places to Eat

1. L'Ambroisie

📍 R3 🏠 9 Pl des Vosges, 75004 🚫 Sun, Mon 🌐 ambroisie-paris.com · €€€

The finest service matches the best food and wine. The chocolate tart is out of this world. Reserve ahead.

2. Marché des Enfants Rouges

📍 R1 🏠 39 Rue de Bretagne, 75003 🚫 Mon 🌐 paris.fr/lieux/marche-couvert-des-enfants-rouges-5461 · €

Food from Morocco to the Caribbean is available at this old covered market. It gets crowded at weekends but is perfect for lunch during the week.

3. Carette

📍 G4 🏠 25 Pl des Vosges, 75003 📞 01 48 87 94 07 · €€

Salads and sandwiches, as well as delicious cakes, feature at this lovely patisserie and tea room on the picturesque Place des Vosges (p95).

4. Chez Paul

📍 H5 🏠 13 Rue de Charonne, 75011 🌐 chezpaul.com · €€

An old-style bistro with a simple but delicious menu and excellent wine list. Reserve your table ahead.

Chez Paul's vintage-chic dining room with tiled floors

5. Le Clown Bar

📍 H4 🏠 114 Rue Amelot, 75011 🌐 clownbar.fr · €€€

Inventive dishes and natural wines served in a circus-themed, Art Nouveau setting. Try the meaty *pithiviers* (pies).

6. Breizh Café

📍 G4 🏠 109 Rue Vieille du Temple, 75003 🌐 breizhcafe.com · €€

An award-winning crêperie offering savoury and sweet Breton pancakes. The selection of buckwheat galettes includes daily specials.

7. Le Baron Rouge

📍 H5 🏠 1 Rue Théophile Roussel, 75012 🚫 Mon 🌐 lebaronrouge.net · €

Cold meats, cheeses and oysters are served in an authentic setting next to Marché d'Aligre (p73).

8. Le Temps des Cerises

📍 R4 🏠 31 Rue de la Cerisaie, 75004 🌐 letempsdescerises-restaurant.fr · €€

One of the oldest restaurants in Paris, serving bacon-wrapped scallops, escargot and a selection of desserts.

9. Septime

📍 H5 🏠 80 Rue de Charonne, 75011 🌐 septime-charonne.fr · €€€

Dishes such as cress-and-sorrel risotto and veal tartare are served at this Michelin-starred bistro. Book ahead.

10. L'As du Fallafel

📍 Q3 🏠 34 Rue des Rosiers, 75004 📞 01 48 87 63 60 🚫 Fri D, Sat · €

This is one of the best falafel joints in the city. The special with aubergine and spicy sauce is a must.

TUILERIES AND OPÉRA QUARTERS

These two quarters were once the province of the rich and the royal, and there's still an undeniable air of luxury about them. The first area encompasses the Jardin des Tuileries and its surrounds. Among the most famous green spaces in Paris, the garden is bookended by the fascinating Louvre and the historic Place de la Concorde. To the north, the grand Opera House gives the second quarter its name. Witnessing one of the many ballet and dance performances, concerts or operas hosted here is a sensory delight – as is admiring the building's sumptuous architecture. This pretty area is also lined by broad avenues and dotted with theatres.

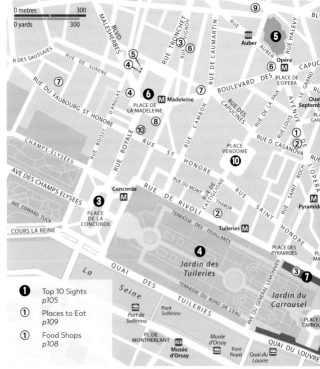

- **1** Top 10 Sights p105
- **1** Places to Eat p109
- **1** Food Shops p108

For places to stay in this area, see p177

1 Musée du Louvre

The world's most visited museum, the Louvre *(p22)* houses a stirring collection of art, including the *Mona Lisa*, along with antiquities from the Middle East, Egypt, Greece and Rome.

2 Rue de Rivoli
◫ M2

Commissioned by Napoleon and named for his victory over the Austrians at Rivoli in 1797, this grand street links the Louvre with the Champs-Élysées *(p113)*. Along one side, railings have replaced the old Tuileries walls, opening up the view. Opposite, striking Neo-Classical apartments sit atop the long arcades. Since 2020 cars have been banned and bike lanes added, making strolling the street a pleasant experience.

Ornate Maritime Fountain and the Luxor obelisk, Place de la Concorde

3 Place de la Concorde
◫ D3

This historic octagonal square, covering over 8 ha (20 acres), was built between 1755 and 1775 as the setting for a statue of Louis XV; by 1792 it had become the Place de la Révolution and its central monument was the guillotine. Louis XVI, Marie-Antoinette and more than 1,000 others were executed here. In 1795, in the spirit of reconciliation, it received its present name. The central obelisk, 23 m (75 ft) tall and covered in hieroglyphics, is from a 3,300-year-old Luxor temple, and was a gift from Egypt, erected in 1833. Two fountains and eight statues represent French cities. On the north side of the square are the Hôtel de la Marine and Hôtel Crillon.

4 Jardin des Tuileries
◫ J2

These gardens *(p60)* were first laid out as part of the old Tuileries Palace, built for Catherine de Médici in 1564 but burned down in 1871. André Le Nôtre redesigned them into formal French gardens in 1664. At the Louvre end is the Arc de Triomphe du Carrousel (1808). Also here is an underground shopping centre, the Carrousel du Louvre. Nearby, sensuous sculptures by Aristide Maillol (1861–1944) adorn the ornamental pools and walkways. At the far end are the Jeu de Paume *(p57)* and the Musée de l'Orangerie *(p56)*, famous for its giant canvases of Monet waterlilies.

Stunning Baroque details and mosaics in the Palais Garnier

5 Palais Garnier

📍 E2 📍 Pl de l'Opéra, 75009
🕐 10am–5pm daily 🌐 operade
paris.fr ↗

Designed by Charles Garnier for Napoleon III in 1862, Paris's opulent opera house took 13 years to complete. A range of styles from Classical to Baroque incorporates stone friezes and columns, statues and a green copper cupola. The ornate interior has a grand staircase, mosaic domed ceiling over the grand foyer and an auditorium with a ceiling by Marc Chagall. There's even an underground lake – the inspiration for Gaston Leroux's *Phantom of the Opera* – sadly closed to visitors. The opera house can only be visited via pre-booked timed slots.

6 Place de la Madeleine

📍 D3 🌐 lamadeleineparis.fr

Surrounded by 52 Corinthian columns, the Classical Madeleine church *(p52)* commands this elegant square. On the east side a colourful flower market takes place from Monday to Saturday. Around the square are some of the most upmarket *épiceries* (food stores) and speciality shops in the city.

7 Musée des Arts Décoratifs

📍 M2 📍 107 Rue de Rivoli, 75001 🕐 11am–6pm Tue–Sun (temporary exhibitions: to 9pm Thu) 🌐 madparis.fr ↗

This huge collection covers the decorative arts from the Middle Ages to the 20th century. With more than 100 rooms, its highlights include the Medieval and Renaissance galleries, the Art Deco rooms and a superb jewellery collection. There are also displays of fashion, textiles, posters and advertising ephemera showcased in permanent and temporary exhibits.

8 Galerie Vivienne and Galerie Colbert

📍 E3 🕐 Daily; hours vary, check website 🌐 passagesetgaleries.fr

These two covered arcades dating from the 19th century are arguably the most beautiful of the few remaining passages in Paris. Built to rival each other, both feature frescoed floors and elegant lighting fixtures that enthral visitors. Today, Galerie Vivienne *(4 Rue des Petits Champs, 75002)* houses shops and cafés frequented by the students at the University of Paris, including Librairie Jousseaume, a second-hand bookshop. Galerie Colbert *(4 Rue Vivienne, 75002)* has no shops, but it houses cultural institutions and a lovely glass rotunda.

9 Domaine National du Palais-Royal

🚇 L1 🚏 8 Rue Montpensier, 75001 🕐 Gardens and arcades: Apr–Sep: 8:30am–10:30pm daily; Oct–Mar: 8am–8:30pm daily 🔒 Palace: to the public 🌐 domaine-palais-royal.fr

In the late 18th century extensive changes were made to the Palais Royal complex under the dukes of Orléans. The architect Victor Louis was commissioned to build 60 uniformly styled houses around three sides of the square and the adjacent theatre, which now houses the Comédie-Française (p66). Today the arcades house specialist shops, galleries and restaurants, and the courtyard and gardens contain modern works of art.

10 Place Vendôme

🚇 E3

Jules Hardouin-Mansart, the architect of Versailles (p159), designed the elegant façades of this royal square for Louis XIV in 1698. It was originally intended for foreign embassies, but bankers soon moved in and built lavish dwellings. It remains home to jewellers and financiers today. The world-famous Ritz hotel was established here at the turn of the 20th century. The column, topped by a statue of Napoleon, is a replica of the one destroyed by the Commune in 1871.

Napoleon's commemorative column in Place Vendôme

A DAY IN THE TUILERIES

Morning

Visiting the **Louvre** (p22) takes planning, and you should pre-book a timed entry slot online or in person at the ticket desk. Pick up a map as you enter so that you don't miss the main highlights. Enjoy a morning coffee in an elegant café in the Richelieu or Denon wings within the museum.

From the Louvre, either take a quick detour to Buren's columns in the **Jardin du Palais-Royal** (p60) or stroll west along **Rue de Rivoli** (p105). Turn right onto Rue Rouget de Lisle and walk to the bottom to reach **Da Rosa Jr.**, a creative little bistro (17 Rue Rouget de Lisle; darosajr.com).

Afternoon

Get some fresh air in the **Jardin des Tuileries** (p105) then walk down to **Place de la Madeleine** to spend the afternoon browsing in its many gourmet stores, or visit the **Galerie Vivienne** and **Galerie Colbert**. Later, take tea in the café of one of the best shops, **Fauchon** (p72). Walk down through **Place de la Concorde** (p105) towards the 18th-century **Pont de la Concorde** to take in the views over the Seine. Look west towards the **Eiffel Tower** (p34) to catch a spectacular sunset panorama. Finish the day with a gastronomic dinner at two-Michelin-starred **Le Meurice** (p109).

Food Shops

A wide range of macarons at Pierre Hermé

1. Pierre Hermé
🗺 E3 🏠 39 Ave de l'Opéra, 75002
Follow the rainbow of exquisite macarons in classic and more intriguing flavours at this shop.

2. Cedric Grolet Opéra
🗺 E3 🏠 35 Ave de l'Opéra, 75002
Award-winning *pâtissier* Cedric Grolet's stunning cakes and fruit tarts appear as art against the minimalist decor of his shop.

3. Marquise de Sévigné
🗺 D3 🏠 16 Rue Tronchet, 75008
Chocolates and *dragées* (sugar-coated almonds) are the speciality at this haven for those with a sweet tooth.

4. Caviar Kaspia
🗺 D3 🏠 17 Pl de la Madeleine, 75008
The peak of indulgence. Choose from caviars from around the world, plus smoked eel, salmon and other fishy fare along with a wide range of vodkas. Try an amazing baked potato with caviar in the upstairs dining room.

5. La Maison de la Truffe
🗺 D3 🏠 19 Pl de la Madeleine, 75008
France's finest black truffles are sold here during the winter. Preserved truffles and other delicacies can be savoured in the shop or at home.

6. La Maison du Miel
🗺 D3 🏠 24 Rue Vignon, 75009
The "house of honey", family owned since 1908, is the place to try speciality honeys, to spread on your toast or your body in the form of soaps and oils.

7. La Maison du Chocolat
🗺 E3 🏠 8 Blvd de la Madeleine, 75009
A superb chocolate shop offers fine chocolates and exquisite patisserie including eclairs, tarts and mouthwatering macarons.

8. Maille
🗺 D3 🏠 6 Pl de la Madeleine, 75008
The retail outlet for one of France's finest mustard-makers. Fresh mustard is served in lovely ceramic jars. and seasonal limited-edition mustards are also available.

9. Galeries Lafayette Le Gourmet
🗺 E2 🏠 35 Blvd Haussmann, 75009
Galeries Lafayette's luxurious food hall has an array of breads, pastries, chocolate, wines and other treats, as well as an in-store café and dining counters.

10. Ladurée Paris Royale
🗺 D3 🏠 16 Rue Royale, 75008
This splendid belle époque tea salon has been serving some of the best macarons in Paris since 1862.

Delightful chocolate sculptures at La Maison du Chocolat

Café de la Paix's outdoor covered patio packed with diners

Places to Eat

1. Café Marly

🗺 E4 🏠 93 Rue de Rivoli, 75001
🌐 cafe-marly.com · €€

This enchanting brasserie overlooks the glass pyramid of the Louvre and offers a creative menu.

2. Le Meurice Alain Ducasse

🗺 E3 🏠 228 Rue de Rivoli, 75001
🔒 Sat & Sun, Aug 🌐 alainducasse-meurice.com · €€€

Sample delectable dishes at Alain Ducasse's two-Michelin-starred venue.

3. Loulou

🗺 M2 🏠 107 Rue de Rivoli, 75001
📞 01 42 60 41 96 · €€€

The Musée des Arts Décoratifs' stylish French-Italian restaurant has beautiful views of the Louvre from its *terrasse*.

4. Lucas Carton

🗺 D3 🏠 9 Pl de la Madeleine, 75008
🔒 Sun & Mon, Aug, public hols
🌐 lucascarton.com · €€€

Chef Hugo Bourny takes the reins at one of Paris's oldest gourmet restaurants. The food is superb.

5. Caffè Stern

🗺 F3 🏠 47 Passage des Panoramas, 75002 🌐 alajmo.it/en/pages/menu-caffe-stern · €€€

Housed in a historic arcade, this Italian restaurant uses seasonal ingredients and supports small-scale wineries.

6. Café de la Paix

🗺 E3 🏠 5 Pl de l'Opéra, 75009
🌐 cafedelapaix.fr · €€€

Step back in time at this gourmet restaurant, which first opened its doors in 1862. The café has a beautiful frescoed interior and the menu features seasonal produce.

7. Jean-François Piège – Le Grand Restaurant

🗺 D3 🏠 7 Rue Aguesseau, 75008
🌐 jeanfrançoispiege.com · €€€

This chic restaurant with striking and elegant interiors serves modern French cuisine.

8. Kunitoraya

🗺 E3 🏠 41 Rue de Richelieu, 75001 🔒 Sun
🌐 palaisroyalrestaurant.com · €

There's often a queue at this bustling udon bar serving perfect noodles in a rich broth. A larger sister restaurant is along the road at No 5.

9. Restaurant du Palais Royal

🗺 E3 🏠 110 Galerie de Valois, 75001
📞 01 40 20 00 27 🔒 Sat & Sun · €€€

Contemporary French food is served in the bucolic setting of the Jardin du Palais-Royal *(p60)*.

10. Verjus

🗺 E3 🏠 52 Rue de Richelieu, 75001
🔒 Sat–Mon 🌐 verjusparis.com · €€€

Book ahead for the set six-course gourmet dinner in the dining room, but you can simply turn up for a lighter bite in the wine bar *(47 Rue Montpensier)*.

Clockwise from top
The stunning auditorium of the Palais Garnier; the opulently decorated Grand Foyer; the building's intricately sculpted façade

CHAMPS-ÉLYSÉES

The Champs-Élysées is the most famous street in Paris and the quarter that lies around it radiates wealth and power. Once little more than open fields on the outskirts of Paris, the avenue transformed into a fashionable locality after the nobility began building townhouses here in the 18th century. Today, it is home to the president of France, embassies and haute couture fashion houses, as well as five-star hotels and high-end restaurants. The Champs-Élysées runs from Place de la Concorde to Place Charles de Gaulle, and it's here that France celebrates national events, holds victory celebrations, parades and protests, or mourns at the funeral cortèges of the great and the good.

❶	Top 10 Sights p113
①	Places to Eat p119
①	Designer Shops p118
①	International Connections p116

For places to stay in this area, see p177

Looking down the Avenue des Champs-Élysées from the Arc de Triomphe

1 Arc de Triomphe

Commissioned by Napoleon after his victory in the Battle of Austerlitz in 1805, the Arc de Triomphe (p38) has been a symbol of the country ever since. It was from here, on 26 August 1944, that de Gaulle lead the historic parade marking the liberation of Paris.

2 Avenue des Champs-Élysées

C3

One of the most famous avenues in the world came into being when the royal gardener André Le Nôtre planted an arbour of trees here in 1667. In the mid-19th century it acquired pedestrian paths, fountains, gas lights and cafés, and became a hot spot for socializing and entertainment. Today, the avenue hosts city events and state processions. It is car-free on the first Sunday of every month, allowing visitors to experience it without any traffic. The Rond-Point des Champs-Élysées is the prettiest part, with chestnut trees and flower-beds. A walk along this thoroughfare is an essential Paris experience.

3 Grand Palais

D3 **3** Ave du Général-Eisenhower, 75008 **For renovations until 2025** **grandpalais.fr**

This vast belle époque exhibition hall was built for the Universal Exhibition in 1900. Its splendid glass roof is a landmark of the Champs-Élysées. The façade is a mix of Art Nouveau, Neo-Classical and mosaic details, with bronze horses and chariots at the four corners of the roof. It is closed for renovations, but a temporary exhibition has been set up in the Champ de Mars.

4 Place Charles de Gaulle

C3 **Ave des Champs-Élysées, 75008**

Known as the Place de l'Étoile until Charles de Gaulle's death in 1969, the area is still referred to simply as l'Étoile, "the star". Motorists should be cautious as traffic laws don't really apply here.

Neo-Classical Petit Palais, topped with cherubic statues

5 Petit Palais

D3 **Ave Winston Churchill, 75008** **10am–6pm Tue–Sun (exhibitions: to 8pm Fri & Sat)** **1 Jan, 1 May, 14 Jul, 25 Dec** **petitpalais.paris.fr**

The "little palace" echoes its iconic neighbour, the Grand Palais, in style. It is graced with Ionic columns and a dome. The palace was initially built for the Universal Exhibition in 1900, but now it houses the Musée des Beaux Arts de la Ville de Paris. The wing close to the river is used for temporary exhibitions, while the Champs-Élysées side of the palace houses the permanent collections featuring Greek and Roman artifacts, Renaissance clocks and jewellery, and furniture from the 17th, 18th and 19th centuries.

6 Pont Alexandre III

D3

Built for the 1900 Universal Exhibition to carry visitors over the Seine to the Grand and Petit Palais, this bridge (p58) is a superb example of the steel architecture and ornate Art Nouveau style popular at the time. Named after Alexander III of Russia, who laid the foundation stone, its decoration displays both Russian and French heraldry. The bridge creates a fine thoroughfare from the Champs-Elysées to the Hôtel des Invalides.

7 Rue du Faubourg St-Honoré

D3

Running parallel to the Champs-Élysées, this is Paris's equivalent of fashionable Fifth Avenue, Bond Street or Rodeo Drive. From Saint Laurent and Givenchy to Gucci and Hermès, the shopfronts read like a *Who's Who* of fashion. Even if the prices may be out of reach, window-shopping is fun. There are also elegant antiques and art galleries. Look out for swallows that nest on the 19th-century façades.

8 Avenue Montaigne

C3

In the 19th century the Avenue Montaigne was a nightlife hotspot. Parisians danced the night away at the Mabille Dance Hall until it closed in 1870 and Adolphe Sax made music with his newly invented saxophone in the Winter Garden. Today this chic avenue is the most fashionable street and a rival to the Rue du Faubourg St-Honoré as it is home to more haute couture houses, such as Christian Dior and Valentino. There are also luxury hotels, restaurants, popular cafés, and the Comédie des Champs-Élysées and Théâtre des Champs-Élysées.

9 Palais de l'Elysée

D3 ⬛ 55 Rue du Faubourg St-Honoré, 75008 ⬛ To the public

Built in 1718, this elegant palace was turned into a dance hall after the Revolution, then, in the 19th century, it became the residence of Napoleon's sister Caroline Murat, followed by his wife Empress Josephine. His nephew, Napoleon III, also lived here while plotting his 1851 coup. Since 1873 it has been the home of the president of France. For this reason, the palace guards don't like people getting too close to the building.

10 Musée Jacquemart-André

C2 ⬛ 158 Blvd Haussmann, 75008 ⬛ Hours vary, chech website ⬛ musee-jacquemart-andre.com ⬛

This fine display of art and furniture, once belonging to collectors Edouard André and his wife Nélie Jacquemart, is housed in a late-19th-century mansion. It is known for its Italian Renaissance works, including frescoes by Tiepolo and Paolo Uccello's *St George and the Dragon* (c. 1435). The reception rooms feature paintings by François Boucher and Jean-Honoré Fragonard. A lovely period tearoom overlooks the gardens.

Impressive tapestries at the Musée Jacquemart-André

A DAY OF SHOPPING

Morning

The Champs-Élysées area is a good place for leisurely walks. Start the morning strolling the grounds of the **Petit Palais**.

Head to the **Avenue Montaigne** for window-shopping – Prada and Dior, among others, have flagship stores here. Take a break in the **Bar des Théâtres** (*44 Rue Jean Goujon; closed Sun D*), where fashion names and the theatre crowd from the Comédie des Champs-Élysées hang out.

Call ahead for a table at **Le Cinq** (*p119*) to splurge on lunch, and head up the **Avenue George V**, lined with luxury boutiques including Armani and Kenzo, and truly eye-catching grande-dame hotels.

Afternoon

Walk along the **Champs-Élysées** (*p113*), with French chanteur Joe Dassin's jaunty 1969 tune in mind. You'll find flagship stores of high-end brands here, along with luxury car showrooms and fast-food outlets.

For tea and cakes en route, **Ladurée Paris Royale** (*p108*) is an elegant experience.

Take the underpass to the **Arc de Triomphe** (*p38*) and climb to the top to admire Baron Haussmann's star-shaped town grid and other views, which are superb at dusk when the avenues light up.

International Connections

1. Avenue de Marigny
C3
Renowned American author John Steinbeck lived here for five months in 1954 and described Parisians as "the luckiest people in the world".

2. 8 Rue Artois
C2
In September 2001, legendary Belgian mobster François Vanverbergh – godfather of the French Connection gang – fell victim to a drive-by assassin here as he took his afternoon mineral water.

3. 37 Avenue Montaigne
C3
Having wowed Paris with her comeback performances, iconic German actress and singer Marlene Dietrich spent her reclusive final years in a luxury apartment on this street.

4. Pont de l'Alma
C3
Diana, Princess of Wales, died in an accident in the underpass here in 1997. Her unofficial memorial, the Liberty Flame *(p58)* attracts thousands of visitors each year.

5. 31 Avenue George V, Hôtel George V
C3
A roll-call of rockers – from the Rolling Stones and Jim Morrison to J-Lo and Madonna – have made this hotel their regular Paris home-from-home.

A portrait of famous French novelist, Marcel Proust

6. 102 Boulevard Haussmann
D2
Hypochondriac author Marcel Proust lived in a cork-lined room – on display in the Musée Carnavalet *(p96)* – penning his masterpiece: *In Search of Lost Time*.

7. 37 Avenue George V
C3
Franklin D. Roosevelt and his new bride Eleanor visited his aunt's apartment here in 1905. He was later commemorated in the name of a nearby avenue.

8. 49 Avenue des Champs-Élysées
C3
Author Charles Dickens may well have had "the best of times and the worst of times" when he resided here during the winter of 1855–6. Ten years earlier he had also lived at 38 Rue de Courcelles.

9. 114 Avenue des Champs-Élysées
C2
Brazilian aviation pioneer Alberto Santos-Dumont planned many aeronautical feats – notably that of circling the Eiffel Tower in 1901 – from here.

10. Hôtel Elysée-Palace
C3
Mata Hari, the Dutch spy and dancer, set up her lair in Room 113 before finally being arrested at 25 Avenue Montaigne.

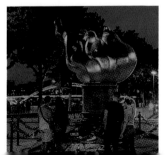

Memorial to Princess Diana at Pont de l'Alma

Events on the Champs-Élysées

1. 1616
Paris's grand avenue was first laid out when Marie de Médici, wife of Henri IV, had a carriage route, the Cours-la-Reine (Queen's Way), constructed through the marshland along the Seine.

2. 1667
Landscape gardener André Le Nôtre lengthened the Jardin des Tuileries (p105) to meet the Cours-la-Reine, and opened up the view with a double row of chestnut trees, creating what was called the Grand Cours.

3. 1709
The avenue was renamed the Champs-Élysées (Elysian Fields). In Greek mythology, the Elysian Fields were the "place of ideal happiness", the abode of the blessed after death.

4. 1724
The Duke of Antin, overseer of the royal gardens, extended the avenue to the heights of Chaillot, the present site of the Arc de Triomphe (p38).

5. 26 August 1944
Parisians celebrated the liberation of the city from Nazi Occupation with triumphant processions and festivities.

6. 30 May 1968
The infamous demonstrations of May 1968 took place here when student protests against the state led to massive gatherings and riots. De Gaulle and his supporters held a huge counter-demonstration on the Champs-Élysées, marking a turning point in the uprising.

7. 12 November 1970
The death of President Charles de Gaulle was an immense event in France, as he had been a dominant political figure for 30 years. He was honoured with a silent parade along the Champs-Élysées.

8. 14 July 1989
The parade on Bastille Day marking the bicentennial of the Revolution was a dazzling display of folk culture and avant-garde theatre. It was a distinct change from the usual military events, and was organized by Mitterrand's Culture Minister, Jack Lang.

9. 8 May 2016
In a series of environmentally friendly measures, the mayor of Paris decreed that the Champs-Élysées would be car-free on the first Sunday of each month, starting May 2016. This also allows pedestrians to experience the beautiful avenue without traffic.

10. July 2024
In celebration of the 2024 Olympic Games, the Place Charles de Gaulle was turned into an "extraordinary garden". As part of Mayor Hidalgo's plans, traffic lanes were reduced and visitors to the arch were also given more space to admire the spectacle.

The monumental Arc de Triomphe on the Champs-Élysées

French designer Barbara Bui's luxury fashion store

Designer Shops

1. Chanel
C3 51 Ave Montaigne, 75008
Chanel classics, from the braided tweed jackets to two-toned shoes, as well as Lagerfeld's more daring designs, are displayed in this branch of the main Rue Cambon store.

2. Christian Dior
C3 30–32 Ave Montaigne, 75008
The grey and white decor, with silk bows on chairs, makes a chic backdrop for fashions from lingerie to evening wear.

3. Givenchy
C3 28 Rue du Faubourg St-Honoré, 75008
This famous fashion house has been synonymous with Parisian style since the 1930s. Shop for women's and men's ready-to-wear outfits here.

4. Balenciaga
C3 57 Ave Montaigne, 75008
This world-famous label is known for its audacious yet memorable modern creations, which are now designed by Demna Gvasalia.

5. Hermès
C3 24 Rue du Faubourg St-Honoré, 75008
Head to this well-known luxury brand for timeless chic apparel, handbags and accessories. Shop for beautiful silk scarves here.

6. Prada
C3 10 Ave Montaigne, 75008
The iconic Italian designer's stylish boutique displays clothes and accessories from the latest collection.

7. Jil Sander
C3 2 Ave Montaigne, 75008
A minimal and modern store, just like the clothes it sells. Sander's trouser suits, cashmere dresses and overcoats in neutral colours are displayed over two floors.

8. Chloé
C3 50 Ave Montaigne, 75008
Simple, classy, ready-to-wear designer women's clothes and accessories are sold in this minimalist temple to feminine chic.

9. Eres
C3 40 Ave Montaigne, 75008
A range of luxury but understated swimwear and lingerie, in subtle colours, is beautifully displayed in this elegant boutique. Everything has a certain Parisian sensuality.

10. Barbara Bui
C3 50 Ave Montaigne, 75008
High-end Parisian fashion designer Barbara Bui has been creating elegant womenswear and accessories since the 1980s. Her collection is made from colourful, luxury fabrics.

Places to Eat

1. La Relais Plaza

C3 Plaza Athénée, 21 Ave Montaigne, 75008 dorchester collection.com · €€€

Replacing Alain Ducasse in 2021, celebrity chef Jean Imbert brings a gourmet twist to classic brasserie fare in this fabled Art Deco dining room.

2. Le Jardin du Petit Palais

D3 Petit Palais, Ave Winston Churchill, 75008 Mon, 1 Jan, 1 May, 14 Jul, 25 Dec petitpalais.paris.fr · €

Take a light lunch in the casual café of the Petit Palais, which opens onto a charming enclosed garden.

3. Le Mermoz

C3 16 Rue Jean Mermoz, 75008 Sat & Sun lemermozparis.fr · €€€

Le Mermoz brings a creative approach to bistro cuisine. It offers a three-course lunch and small plates.

4. Bellota Bellota

C3 11 Rue Clément Marot, 75008 Sun bellota-bellota.com · €

This intimate tapas bar and Spanish deli serves excellent tapas, luxurious *jamón ibérico* and Spanish wine.

5. Pierre Gagnaire

C3 6 Rue Balzac, 75008 Sat, Sun, Aug, 1 weeh Dec–Jan pierre gagnaire.com· €€€

Celebrated for his artistry in blending flavours, Pierre Gagnaire creates

Oak-panelling adorning the interior of L'Épicerie

culinary magic at this modern Michelin-starred French diner – often with produce he's grown himself.

6. L'Épicerie

D2 112 Rue du Faubourg St-Honoré, 75008 oethercollec tion.com · €€€

In Hôtel Le Bristol's elegant dining room or on the garden terrace, diners can choose from chef Eric Frechon's three-Michelin-starred menu.

7. Taillevent

C3 15 Rue Lamennais, 75008 Sat & Sun, Aug letaillevent.com · €€€

The menu at this haute-cuisine spot, housed in a 19th-century mansion, changes often, relying on fresh, seasonal ingredients. Book ahead.

8. Le 116

B3 2 Rue Auguste Vacquerie, 75116 01 47 20 10 45 · €€

Wagyu beef burgers and excellent cocktails are on the menu at this off-shoot of the Michelin-starred Pages.

9. L'Atelier des Chefs

D2 10 Rue de Penthièvre, 75008 Mon atelierdeschefs.fr · €

This cooking school offers a range of classes in French and you get to eat the meal you've made after a session.

10. Le Cinq

C3 31 Ave George V, 75008 fourseasons.com · €€€

The George V's *(p116)* three-Michelin-starred restaurant serves French cuisine with a modern twist.

CHAILLOT

Chaillot was a separate village until the 19th century, when it was swallowed up by the growing city and bestowed with wide avenues and grand mansions, many of which now house embassies. The quarter's centrepiece is the glorious Palais de Chaillot, its white-stone wings embracing the Jardins du Trocadéro and its terrace facing the Eiffel Tower, across the Seine. Behind the palace is Place du Trocadéro, laid out in 1858 and ringed with smart cafés.

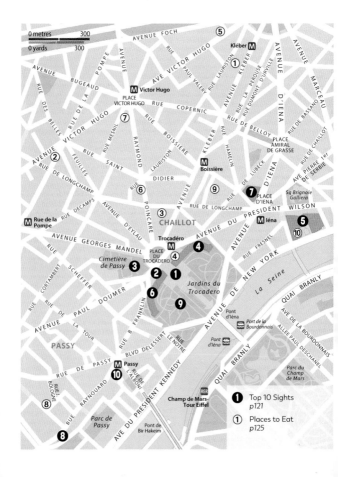

Aerial view of the Palais de Chaillot from the Eiffel Tower

1 Palais de Chaillot
B4 **1 Pl du Trocadéro et du 11 Novembre**

The fall of his empire scuppered Napoleon's plans for a palace for his son on Chaillot hill, but the site was later used for the Trocadéro Palace, built for the Universal Exhibition of 1878. It was replaced by the present Neo-Classical building with its colonnaded wings for the pre-war exhibition of 1937. The two pavilions house three museums, including the Musée de l'Homme. The broad terrace is the domain of souvenir sellers and skateboarders by day, while at night tourists come to admire the splendid view of the Eiffel Tower across the Seine. Two bronzes, *Apollo* by Henri Bouchard and *Hercules* by Pommier, stand at the front of the terrace. Beneath the terrace is the 1,200-seat Théâtre National de Chaillot.

2 Musée National de la Marine de Paris
B4 **17 Pl du Trocadéro et du 11 Novembre, 75116** **11am–7pm Wed–Mon** **musee-marine.fr**

The National Marine Museum traces France's maritime history through a collection of 1,000 restored pieces, among them model ships and diving suits. It features wonderfully exact scale models (most of them two centuries old), mementos of naval heroes, paintings and navigational instruments. While

visiting, take note of the museum's scent, which has been customized to replicate the smell of the sea.

3 Cimetière de Passy
A4 **Pl du Trocadéro (entrance Rue du Commandant Schloesing), 75016**

This small cemetery established in 1820 covers only 1 ha (2.5 acres), yet many famous people have been laid to rest here *(p124)* with the Eiffel Tower as their eternal view. It is worth a visit just to admire the striking sculptures on the tombs.

4 Cité de l'Architecture et du Patrimoine
B4 **Palais de Chaillot, 75116** **11am–7pm Wed–Mon (to 9pm Thu)** **citedelarchitecture.fr**

This museum is an ode to French architectural heritage, showcasing its development through the ages. The Galerie des Moulages (medieval to Renaissance) contains moulded portions of churches and French cathedrals including Chartres. The Galerie d'Architecture Moderne et Contemporaine includes a reconstruction of an apartment designed by Le Corbusier, and architectural designs from 1990 onwards. The gallery in the Pavillon de Tête has a collection of murals copied from medieval frescoes. Book in advance.

5 Musée d'Art Moderne de la Ville de Paris

📍 B4 📍 11 Ave du Président Wilson, 75116 🕐 10am–6pm Tue–Sun (temporary exhibitions: to 9:30pm Thu) 📅 Public hols 🌐 mam.paris.fr 🔗

This museum is housed in the east wing of the Palais de Tokyo (p57), built for the 1937 World's Fair. Its permanent collection consists of 10,000 works and includes such masters as Chagall, Picasso, Modigliani and Léger; further highlights include Raoul Dufy's huge mural The Spirit of Electricity (1937) and Picabia's Lovers (After the Rain) (1925). The museum also showcases the work of up-and-coming artists in the west wing. An admission fee is applicable for temporary exhibitions.

6 Musée de l'Homme

📍 B4 📍 17 Pl du Trocadéro, 75016 🕐 11am–7pm Wed–Mon 📅 1 Jan, 1 May, 14 Jul, 25 Dec 🌐 museedelhomme.fr 🔗

This anthropological and ethnographic museum, opened in 1938 and renovated in 2010–15, uses scientific and cultural approaches to explore the biggest questions surrounding the human race. Home to one of the world's most comprehensive prehistoric collections, it traces the history of humankind and addresses the questions, who are we, where do we come from and what is our future? Fossils, skulls, anthropological casts and other displays help visitors understand their biological evolution as well as the development of societies and cultures over the centuries.

7 Musée National des Arts Asiatiques–Guimet

📍 B3 📍 6 Pl d'Iéna, 75116 🕐 10am–6pm Wed–Mon 📅 1 Jan, 1 May, 25 Dec 🌐 guimet.fr 🔗

Founded in 1889, Musée National des Arts Asiatiques–Guimet is one of the world's foremost museums of Asian art, and the largest European museum devoted to the subject. The Khmer Buddhist temple sculptures from Angkor Wat are the highlight of a fine collection of Cambodian art.

Sculptures at the Musée National des Arts Asiatiques–Guimet

Emile Guimet's collection tracing Chinese and Japanese religion from the 4th to 19th centuries is also on display, as are rare artifacts from Afghanistan, India, Indonesia and Vietnam.

8 Maison de Balzac

🗺 A4 📍 47 Rue Raynouard, 75016
🕙 10am–6pm Tue–Sun 🗓 Public hols
🌐 maisondebalzac.paris.fr

The writer Honoré de Balzac rented an apartment here from 1840 to 1847, assuming a false name to avoid his many creditors. He revised his epic series of novels, *La comédie humaine*, here. The house is now a museum displaying first editions and manuscripts, personal mementos and letters, and paintings and drawings of his friends and family. It also houses a café and temporary exhibitions. The museum offers free admission to its permanent exhibitions.

9 Jardins du Trocadéro

🗺 B4

Designed in 1937, the tiered Trocadéro Gardens descend gently down Chaillot hill from the palace to the Seine and the Pont d'Iéna. The centrepiece of this 10-ha (25-acre) park is the long rectangular pool lined with stone and bronze statues, including *Woman* by Daniel Bacqué (1874–1947). Its illuminated fountains (p61) are spectacular when seen at night. With flowering trees, various walkways and bridges over small streams, the Trocadéro Gardens are a romantic place for an evening stroll.

10 Musée du Vin

🗺 A4 📍 5 Square Charles Dickens, Rue des Eaux, 75016 🕙 10am–6pm Tue–Sat 🌐 lemparis.com

The vaulted 14th-century cellars where the monks of Passy once made wine are an atmospheric setting for this wine museum. Waxwork figures recreate the history of the wine-making process, and there are displays of wine paraphernalia. It also has tasting sessions, wine for sale and an excellent restaurant.

A DAY IN CHAILLOT

Morning

Start your day at the **Palais de Chaillot** (p121) and take in its perfect view of the **Eiffel Tower** (p34) across the Seine. Afterwards, explore the tree-lined paths of the **Jardins du Trocadéro**, or tour the fascinating collections of the **Cité de l'Architecture** (p121) or the **Musée de l'Homme** (p122).

Have lunch at the **Café du Trocadéro** (8 Pl du Trocadéro; 01 44 05 37 00; open 7am–2am daily) and watch the comings and goings in the square. For something a little fancier, make a reservation well in advance at the excellent **Étude** (p125).

Afternoon

Take a stroll through the **Cimetière de Passy** (p121), where the extravagant tombstones and statuary speak to the good fortunes of the members of the 19th-century upper class buried here (p124). Or, pop into the **Musée National des Arts Asiatiques–Guimet** for its remarkable Eastern artifacts and artworks – don't miss the stunning Riboud collection of rare textiles from India, Japan, China and Indonesia.

Take tea, with eclairs, at **Café Carette**, back at the Place du Trocadéro (01 47 27 98 85; open 7am–11:30pm daily), or have an unforgettable dinner at the stylish **Le Jules Verne** (p131). Be sure to book a table in advance.

Graves in Cimetière de Passy

1. Edouard Manet
Born in Paris in 1832, Manet became the most notorious artist in the city when works such as *Olympia* and *Le Déjeuner sur l'Herbe (p26)* were first exhibited. He died in Paris in 1883.

2. Claude Debussy
The French composer (1862–1918) achieved fame through works such as *Prélude à l'après-midi d'un faune* and *La mer*, and was regarded as the musical equivalent of the Impressionist painters.

3. Berthe Morisot
The French Impressionist artist was born in Paris in 1841, posed for Edouard Manet and later married his lawyer brother Eugène. One of the mainstays of the Impressionist movement, Morisot died in Paris in 1895.

4. Fernandel
The lugubrious French film actor known as Fernandel was born Fernand Contandin in Marseille in 1903. He made more than 100 films in a career that lasted from 1930 until his death in Paris in 1971.

5. Marie Bashkirtseff
This Russian artist became more renowned as a diarist after her death from tuberculosis in 1884. Despite living for only 24 years she produced 84 volumes of diaries and their posthumous publication created a sensation due to their intimate nature.

6. Marie-Louise Jay
A former Bon Marché shopgirl, Jay founded the historic Parisian department store La Samaritaine with her husband, Ernest Cognacq. The couple's fine art collection forms the heart of the Musée Cognacq-Jay *(p95)*.

7. Comte Emmanuel de Las Cases
Born in 1766, this historian and friend of Napoleon shared the emperor's exile on the island of St Helena and recorded his memoirs. Las Cases himself died in Paris in 1842.

8. Gabriel Fauré
The French composer, probably best known today for his *Requiem*, was a great influence on the music of his time. He died in Paris in 1924, at the age of 79.

9. Octave Mirbeau
The satirical French novelist and playwright was also an art critic and a journalist. Born in 1848, he died in Cheverchemont in 1917 and his body was brought to Passy for burial.

10. Henri Farman
The French aviator was born in Paris in 1874 and died there in 1958. He was the first man to make a circular 1-km (0.5-mile) flight, and the first to fly cross-country in Europe. His gravestone shows him at the controls of a primitive plane.

Tombstone of aviation pioneer Henri Farman

Places to Eat

PRICE CATEGORIES

For a three-course meal for one with half a bottle of wine (or equivalent meal), taxes and extra charges

€ under €30 €€ €30–€50 €€€ over €50

Monsieur Bleu's terrace overlooking the Eiffel Tower

1. Alan Geaam

B2 19 Rue Lauriston, 75016 Sun, Mon restaurant.alangeaam.fr · €€€

In this refined restaurant, Michelin-starred chef Alan Geaam combines classic French cuisine with bright Lebanese flavours to create dishes such as langoustine cooked with *soujouk* spices.

2. Le Stella

A3 133 Ave Victor Hugo, 75116 lestella.fr · €€€

This jovial neighbourhood institution, with an almost retro charm, is a traditional Parisian brasserie in style and atmosphere. Le Stella serves fantastic seafood platters.

3. Mokus l'Ecureuil

B3 116 Ave Kléber, 75016 restaurantmohus.fr · €€

This trendy pizzeria and burger bar is set in an industrial-inspired dining room, complete with neon lights and brick walls. It is a great place for comfort food. The menu also features several options for vegetarians.

4. Girafe

B4 1 Pl du Trocadéro et du 11 Novembre 75016 girafe-restaurant.com · €€€

This 1930s-style restaurant, specializing in fish dishes, has prime views of the Eiffel Tower.

5. Prunier

B3 16 Ave Victor Hugo, 75016 Sun, Mon prunier.com · €€€

Fish dishes reign at Prunier. Its Art Deco interior is dazzling.

6. Bistrot Paul Chêne

B3 123 Rue Lauriston, 75116 Sun, Mon D xn--bistrotpaulchne-3nb.fr · €€

Located near Trocadéro, this typically Parisian bistro offers quality food impeccably served.

7. Le Petit Rétro

B3 5 Rue Mesnil, 75016 Sun petitretro.fr · €€€

This cosy bistro offers *blanquette de veau* and chocolate profiteroles.

8. Le Bistrot des Vignes

B4 1 Rue Jean Bologne, 75016 bistrotdesvignes.fr · €€

An unpretentious little bistro of the type everyone hopes to find in Paris.

9. Étude

B3 14 Rue du Bouquet de Longchamp, 75116 Sat L, Sun, Mon restaurant-etude.fr · €€€

Chef Keisuke Yamagishi perfectly balances Franco-Japanese tasting menus of three to five courses. There's also a well-curated, extensive wine list.

10. Monsieur Bleu

B4 20 Ave de New Yorh, 75116 monsieurbleu-restaurant.com · €€€

A modern brasserie within the Palais de Tokyo, near the Musée d'Art Moderne *(p122)*. The terrace has a stunning view of the Eiffel Tower.

EIFFEL TOWER AND INVALIDES

Giving off an air of grandeur, this area of Paris is known for its monumental buildings, grassy esplanades and wide avenues. The quarter is home to two of Paris's best-known landmarks, the Hôtel des Invalides, whose golden dome dazzles against the sky, and the world-famous Eiffel Tower, whose iron form soars high above the city. To the east of Les Invalides are stately mansions, now converted into embassies, and the French parliament, while alongside the Seine lies Jean Nouvel's striking Musée du Quai Branly – Jacques Chirac. The area is also dotted with countless restaurants, including some Michelin-starred options.

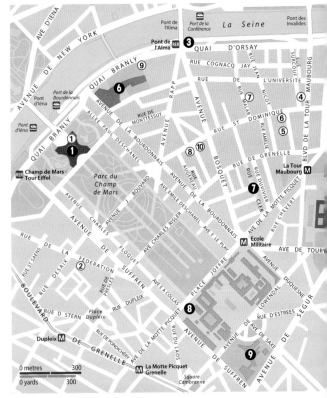

For places to stay in this area, see p178

1 Eiffel Tower

More than seven million visitors a year ascend to the top of the city's landmark (p34) for the spectacular views.

2 Hôtel des Invalides

Founded by Louis XIV, this complex (p46) houses Napoleon's tomb and features various military museums.

3 Musée des Egouts

◘ C4 ◘ Esplanade Habib Bourguiba ◘ 10am–5pm Tue–Sun ◘ musee-egouts.paris.fr ◘◘

The sewers (égouts) of Paris are an incongruously popular attraction. They date from the Second Empire (1851–70), when Baron Haussmann was transforming the city (p10). The sewers, designed by engineer Eugène Belgrand, helped to sanitize and ventilate Paris, and are considered one of Haussmann's finest achievements. The 2,100-km (1,300-mile) network covers the area from Les Halles to La Villette – if laid end-to-end it would stretch from Paris to Istanbul. An hour-long tour includes a walk through some of the tunnels. The museum, which is situated in the sewers beneath the Quai d'Orsay on the Left Bank, tells the story of the city's water and sewers through a range of exhibits and an audio-visual show.

4 Musée de l'Armée

◘ C4 ◘ Hôtel des Invalides, 75007 ◘ 10am–6pm daily (to 10pm first Fri of the month) ◘ 1 Jan, 1 May, 25 Dec ◘ musee-armee.fr ◘

The Army Museum contains one of the largest collections of arms, armour and displays on military history in the world. The range of weapons on display includes examples from prehistoric times to those used during World War II. Housed in the Hôtel des Invalides, the galleries occupy the old refectories in two wings on either side of the courtyard. The museum's ticket price includes entry to the Musée des Plans-Reliefs, the Historial Charles de Gaulle, the Musée de l'Ordre de la Libération and Napoleon's Tomb.

Napoleon's tomb in the crypt of the Musée de l'Armée

5 Musée Rodin

🗺 C4 🚇 77 Rue de Varenne, 75007
🕐 10am–6:30pm Tue–Sun 🔒 1 Jan,
1 May, 25 Dec 🌐 musee-rodin.fr ♿

An impressive collection of works by
Auguste Rodin (1840–1917) is housed
in the 18th-century Hôtel Biron (p130),
where the sculptor and artist spent
the last nine years of his life. The
museum showcases Rodin's prepara-
tory sketches, watercolours, and
bronze and marble masterpieces,
including *The Kiss* and *Eve*. Exhibits
are displayed chronologically and
thematically, showing the creative
processes behind the artist's finished
sculptures – works that arguably paved
the way for modern sculpture. The
Musée Rodin is also home to the third-
largest private garden in Paris, where
works such as *The Thinker*, *Monument
to Balzac* and *The Gates of Hell* stand
amid the lime trees and rose bushes.

6 Musée du Quai Branly – Jacques Chirac

🗺 B4 🚇 37 Quai Jacques Chirac
🕐 10:30am–7pm Tue–Sun (to 10pm
Thu) 🔒 1 May, 25 Dec 🌐 quaibranly.fr ♿

The purpose of this museum is to
showcase the arts of Africa, Asia,
Oceania and the Americas. The collection boasts nearly 300,000 artifacts, of
which 3,500 are on display, including a
fantastic array of African instruments,
Gabonese masks, Aztec statues and
17th-century painted animal hides
from North America (once the pride of
the French royal family). Designed by

YOUNG NAPOLEON

The most famous alumnus of the
École Militaire was Napoleon
Bonaparte, who was admitted as
a cadet, aged 15, in 1784 and was
deemed "fit to be an excellent sailor".
He graduated as a lieutenant in the
artillery, and his passing-out report
stated that "he could go far if the
circumstances are right". The rest,
as they say, is history.

Jean Nouvel, the building is an exhibit
in itself: glass is ingeniously used to
allow the surrounding greenery to act
as a natural backdrop to the collection.

7 Rue Cler

🗺 C4

The pedestrianized cobblestone road
that stretches south of Rue de Grenelle
to Avenue de La Motte-Picquet is the
most exclusive market street in Paris.
Here greengrocers, fishmongers,
butchers and wine merchants sell top-
quality produce to the well-heeled
residents of the area. Tear yourself away
from the mouthwatering displays of
cheeses and pastries, however, to feast
your eyes on the Art Nouveau building
at No 23, also home to a pleasant café.

8 École Militaire

🗺 C5 🚇 21 Pl Joffre, 75007 ♿

At the urging of his mistress Madame
Pompadour, Louis XV approved the
building of the Royal Military Academy
in 1751. Its purpose was to educate 500
sons of impoverished officers. A grand

edifice was designed by Jacques-Ange Gabriel, architect of the Place de la Concorde *(p105)* and the Petit Trianon at Versailles, and completed in 1773. The central pavilion with its quadrangular dome and Corinthian pillars is a splendid example of the French Classical style. The ornate interior is decorated in Louis XVI style; of main interest are the chapel and a Gabriel-designed wrought-iron banister on the main staircase. The massive complex is still in use as a military school today. It is open by special permission only during Journée de la Patrimoine in September. Visitors would need to apply in writing.

9 UNESCO

📍 C5 📍 7 Pl de Fontenoy, 75007
🌐 cultival.fr 📱

The headquarters of the United Nations Educational, Scientific and Cultural Organization (UNESCO) was built in 1958 by an international team of architects from France, Italy and the United States. It is a Y-shaped building of concrete and glass, which showcases 20th-century works by renowned international artists. There is a huge mural by Picasso, ceramics by Joan Miró, and a 2nd-century mosaic from El Djem in Tunisia. Outside is a giant mobile by Alexander Calder and a peaceful Japanese garden. Visits are by appointment only and must be booked online in advance.

10 Assemblée Nationale

📍 D4 📍 126 Rue de l'Université, 75007 🌐 assemblee-nationale.fr 📱

Built for Louis XIV's daughter in 1722, the Palais-Bourbon has housed the lower house of the French parliament since 1827. The Council of the Five Hundred met here during the Revolution, and it was the headquarters of the German Occupation during World War II. You can visit as part of a tour group. Carry your passport and make reservations in advance.

The grandiose Classical façade of the École Militaire

A DAY AROUND THE INVALIDES QUARTER

Morning

Begin the day with a visit to the **Musée Rodin**. A magnificent collection of Rodin's works is displayed both indoors and outside in the attractive garden. Stop for a coffee on the leafy terrace of the garden café.

Alternatively, stroll through the Esplanade des Invalides, with the **Hôtel des Invalides** (p46) as a grand backdrop. Stop in to see **Napoleon's Tomb** (p46) and the **Musée de l'Armée** (p127). Towards the Seine, admire the splendid **Pont Alexandre III** (p114) before heading towards Rue Saint-Dominique for lunch at **Les Cocottes** (p131), top chef Christian Constant's breezy, informal bistro.

Afternoon

After lunch, follow the Rue de l'Université to the **Musée du Quai Branly – Jacques Chirac** and enjoy the collections of tribal art and superb modern architecture. Café Jacques, located in the museum's gardens, is the perfect place to relish a cup of tea.

Make sure you book ahead for a late afternoon visit to the **Eiffel Tower** (p34). The views are spectacular at dusk. Splash out on dinner at **Le Jules Verne** (p131) on level 2, or head back to Musée du Quai Branly – Jacques Chirac's rooftop restaurant, **Les Ombres** (p131). Book in advance for either.

Interior of the Hotel de Villeroy, home to the French Ministry of Agriculture

Mansions

1. Hôtel Biron
Built in 1730, this elegant mansion was transformed into state-owned artists' studios in 1904. Among its residents was Auguste Rodin (1840–1917). After the sculptor's death the house became the Musée Rodin (p128).

2. Hôtel de Villeroy
🗺 D4 🏠 78–80 Rue de Varenne, 75007 🚫 To the public
Built in 1724 for Comédie-Française actress Charlotte Desmarnes, this is now the Ministry of Agriculture.

3. Hôtel de Matignon
🗺 D4 🏠 57 Rue de Varenne, 75007 🚫 To the public
One of the most beautiful mansions in the area is now the official residence of the French prime minister.

4. Hôtel de Boisgelin
🗺 D4 🏠 47 Rue de Varenne, 75007 📞 01 49 54 03 00 (call ahead for appt)
Built in 1732 by Jean Sylvain Cartaud, this mansion has housed the Italian Embassy since 1938.

5. Hôtel de Gallifet
🗺 D4 🏠 50 Rue de Varenne, 75007 🕑 Galleries: 10am–1pm, 3–6pm Mon–Fri
This attractive mansion was built between 1776 and 1792 in Classical style. It now functions as the Italian Cultural Institute.

6. Hôtel d'Estrées
🗺 B5 🏠 79 Rue de Grenelle, 75007 🚫 To the public
Three floors of pilasters feature on the 1713 former Russian embassy. Tsar Nicolas II lived here in 1896. It is now the residence of the Russian ambassador.

7. Hôtel d'Avaray
🗺 B5 🏠 85 Rue de Grenelle, 75007 🚫 To the public
Dating from 1728, this mansion belonged to the Avaray family for nearly 200 years. It is now owned by the Dutch government.

8. Hôtel de Brienne
🗺 D4 🏠 14–16 Rue St Dominique, 75007 🚫 To the public
This mansion houses the Ministry of Defence. Napoleon's mother lived here from 1806 to 1817.

9. Hôtel de Noirmoutiers
🗺 B5 🏠 138–140 Rue de Grenelle, 75007 🚫 To the public
Built in 1724, this was once the army staff headquarters. It now houses ministerial offices.

10. Hôtel de Monaco de Sagan
🗺 D4 🏠 57 Rue St-Dominique, 75007 🚫 To the public
Now the Polish ambassador's house, this stately 1784 mansion served as the British Embassy until 1825.

Places to Eat

1. Le Jules Verne

📍 B4 🏠 2nd Level, Eiffel Tower, 75007
🌐 restaurants-toureiffel.com · €€€

On the second floor of the Eiffel Tower, this superb restaurant blends pared-back decor with a luxurious menu. You'll need to book in advance.

2. Le Casse-Noix

📍 B5 🏠 56 Rue de la Fédération, 75015
🔒 Sat & Sun 🌐 le-cassenoix.fr · €€

A charming restaurant serving classic desserts such as *île flottante* (a poached meringue "island" floating on a "sea" of vanilla custard).

3. Arpège

📍 D4 🏠 84 Rue de Varenne, 75007 🔒 Sat & Sun 🌐 alain-passard.com · €€€

Dishes at this acclaimed spot by chef Alain Passard use produce from the restaurant's biodynamic garden. His signature apple tart is a must-try.

4. David Toutain

📍 D4 🏠 29 Rue Surcouf, 75007 🔒 Sat & Sun 🌐 davidtoutain.com · €€€

Awarded two Michelin stars, Chef David Toutain delivers eclectic cuisine that showcases fine seasonal produce and includes vegetarian dishes. The set lunch menu offers good value.

5. Tomy & Co

📍 C4 🏠 22 Rue Surcouf, 75007 🔒 Sat & Sun 🌐 tomygousset.com · €€€

A warm and welcoming restaurant with beautifully presented, delicious and inventive French cuisine from star chef Tomy Gousset.

6. Thoumieux

📍 C4 🏠 79 Rue St-Dominique, 75007
🔒 Aug 🌐 hotel-thoumieux.com · €€€

Classic brasserie fare, such as tartare of beef and profiteroles, is served in an Art Deco-inspired dining room.

7. L'Ami Jean

📍 C4 🏠 27 Rue Malar, 75007 🔒 Sun & Mon 🌐 lamijean.fr · €€€

Inventive dishes include marinated scallops with ewe's milk cheese.

8. Les Cocottes

📍 C4 🏠 135 Rue St-Dominique, 75007
🌐 lescocottes.paris · €€

Star chef Christian Constant's fun French take on a diner – albeit one that serves lobster bisque.

9. Les Ombres

📍 B4 🏠 27 Quai Branly, 75007
🌐 lesombres-restaurant.com · €€€

Stylish rooftop restaurant offering fine food. At night it's a great spot to watch the Eiffel Tower twinkle.

10. La Fontaine de Mars

📍 C4 🏠 129 Rue St-Dominique, 75007
🌐 fontaine-de-mars.com · €€€

The rich, hearty cuisine of southwest France can be found here, such as cassoulet and duck confit.

**Baked treats at the popular
Thoumieux patisserie**

ST-GERMAIN, LATIN AND LUXEMBOURG QUARTERS

St-Germain-des-Prés is a synonym for Paris's café society, made famous by the writers and intellectuals who held court here in the first half of the 20th century. Cafés, trendy boutiques and art galleries still line the streets and squares. The Latin Quarter has been the scholastic centre of Paris for more than 700 years, and buzzes with student bookshops, crêpe stands, cafés and jazz clubs. The area's western border is the bustling Boulevard St-Michel; to the south is the Jardin du Luxembourg.

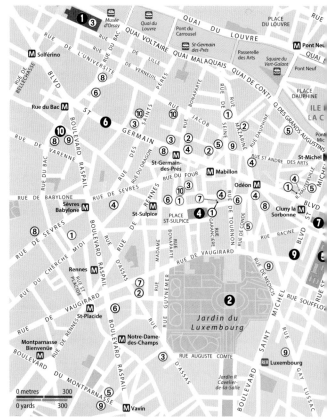

For places to stay in this area, see p178

Lavender in bloom at the Jardin du Luxembourg

1 Musée d'Orsay

The star attraction of this museum (*p26*) is a superb collection of Impressionist art, which includes famous works by Monet, Van Gogh and Degas.

2 Jardin du Luxembourg

📍 L6 ☐ Rue de Médicis–Rue de Vaugirard, 75006 ☐ Dawn–dusk daily

This 25-ha (60-acre) park (*p60*) is set around the Palais du Luxembourg (*p51*). It features the beautiful Medici Fountain (*p61*) and various 19th-century statues, including one of St Geneviève, patron saint of Paris. There is also a children's playground, an open-air café, a bandstand, tennis courts, a puppet theatre and a bee-keeping school.

3 The Panthéon

Paris's Panthéon (*p42*), inspired by the one in Rome, was originally built as a church. Today, it is the final resting place of the nation's great figures.

4 Église St-Sulpice

📍 L5 ☐ 2 Rue Palatine, Pl St-Sulpice, 75006 ☐ 8am–7:45pm daily 🌐 paroissesaintsulpice.paris

The Classical façade of this church features two incongruously matched towers. The two holy water fonts by the front door are made from huge shells given to François I by the Venetian Republic. The restored *Jacob Wrestling with the Angel* and other fine murals by Delacroix (1798–1863) are in the chapel to the right of the main door.

5 La Sorbonne

📍 M5 ☐ 1 Rue Victor Cousin, 75005 ☐ For reserved group tours only 🌐 sorbonne.fr 🔲🔲

This university (*p51*) was founded in 1253 as a theology college for poor students. Philosophers Thomas Aquinas and Roger Bacon taught here; Italian poet Dante, founder of the Jesuits St Ignatius Loyola, and church reformer John Calvin are among its list of alumni. Its tradition for conservatism led to its closure during the Revolution. Book ahead for guided tours.

Elegant shops and boutiques line the Boulevard St-Germain

6 Boulevard St-Germain
❼ J3

This famous Left Bank boulevard runs for more than 3 km (2 miles), anchored by the bridges of the Seine at either end. At its heart is the church of St-Germain-des-Prés, established in 542, although the present church dates from the 11th century. Beyond the famous literary cafés, Flore (p139) and Les Deux Magots (p139), the boulevard runs west past galleries, bookshops and designer boutiques to the Pont de la Concorde. To the east, it cuts across the Latin Quarter, running through the pleasant

JAZZ ON THE LEFT BANK

Jazz has been played in Paris, especially on the Left Bank, since the 1910s. In the 1920s, a great number of black musicians moved here from the US because they found France to be less racially prejudiced than their homeland, and Paris became a second home for many great jazz musicians, such as Sidney Bechet and Albert Nicholas. The city has never lost its love of jazz, nor jazz its love for the city.

street market in the Place Maubert, to join the Pont de Sully, which connects to the Île St-Louis (p80).

7 Musée du Cluny-Musée National du Moyen Age
❼ N5 ❑ 28 Rue du Sommerard, 75005 ❑ 9:30am–6:15pm Tue–Sun ❑ 1 Jan, 1 May, 25 Dec ☒ musee-moyenage.fr ❼

Reopened in 2022 after a major revamp, the Musée du Cluny-Musée National du Moyen Age occupies a mansion built by the abbots of Cluny at the end of the 15th century. It houses a magnificent collection of art, from the Gallo-Roman period to the 15th century. The highlight is the exquisite Lady and the Unicorn tapestry series, representing the five senses. Other displays include beautiful manuscripts, stained-glass windows from the Sainte-Chapelle and 21 carved stone heads of the kings of Judea from Notre-Dame. Incorporated into the museum are the ruins of 2nd-century thermes (Roman baths) with their huge vaulted frigidarium (cold bath). Recitals of medieval music are held regularly at the museum, often at lunchtime on Mondays.

8 Quai de la Tournelle
❼ P5

From this riverbank, just before the Pont de l'Archevêché, there are lovely views across to Notre-Dame. The main attraction of this and the adjacent Quai de Montebello, however, are the dark-green stalls of the *bouquinistes* (p136). The Pont de la Tournelle also offers splendid views up and down the Seine.

9 Musée Maillol

🚇 J4 🏠 59–61 Rue de Grenelle, 75007 🕐 For exhibitions only: 10:30am–6:30pm daily (to 10pm Wed) 🌐 museemaillol.com

Dina Vierny, who modelled for the artist Aristide Maillol (1861–1944) from the age of 15 to 25, went on to set up this foundation located in an 18th-century mansion, dedicated largely to his works. As well as a permanent exhibition of Maillol's varied works, the museum also puts on two temporary exhibitions per year, highlighting a range of modern and contemporary art.

10 Boulevard St-Michel

🚇 M4

The main drag of the Latin Quarter was created in the late 1860s as part of Baron Haussmann's citywide makeover (p10), and named after a chapel that once stood near its northern end. Known for its bustling atmosphere, the boulevard is lined with lively cafés, clothes shops and restaurants. To the east are Rues de la Harpe and de la Huchette, dating back to medieval times. The latter forms an enclave of the city's Greek community, with *souvlaki* stands and Greek restaurants. Place St-Michel was a pivotal spot during both the Nazi occupation and the student riots of 1968. Its huge bronze fountain depicts St Michael slaying Satan.

Statue of St Michael

A DAY ON THE LEFT BANK

Café Campana
L'Atelier de Joël Robuchon
Les Deux Magots
Boulevard St-Germain
Quai de Montebello
Musée Maillol
Café de Flore
Dupin
Shakespeare and Company
Quai de la Tournelle

Morning

Take time to soak up some of that Left Bank atmosphere. Begin on the **Quai de la Tournelle**, strolling by the booksellers here and on the adjacent **Quai de Montebello**, which runs parallel to Rue de la Bûcherie, home to **Shakespeare and Company** (p136).

From here head south down any street away from the river to the busy **Boulevard St-Germain**. Turn right for two famous cafés, **Café de Flore** (p139) and **Les Deux Magots** (p139), and stop for a break at either one, joining the locals talking the morning away.

Then go to the Rue de Grenelle and the **Musée Maillol**, a truly delightful, lesser-known museum. Then enjoy lunch at **Dupin** (p141), a popular bistro that attracts a mix of locals and tourists.

Afternoon

Having pre-booked a timed entry to the **Musée d'Orsay** (p26), spend an hour or two browsing the collections. The most popular works on display are those of the Impressionists, on the upper level.

After exploring the museum, you can rest and enjoy tea and cake in the stylish **Café Campana** (p27) or, if it's dinner time, walk over to **L'Atelier de Joël Robuchon** (p141), having booked in advance, to splurge on the Michelin-starred chef's take on modern French cuisine.

Booksellers

Browsing books at the legendary Shakespeare and Company

1. Shakespeare and Company
◻ N5 ◻ 37 Rue de la Bûcherie, 75005
Bibliophiles spend hours in the rooms and narrow passageways of Paris's renowned English-language book-shop. There are regular author events and readings in English and French. The café next door serves great coffee and cakes.

2. Bouquinistes
◻ N5
The green stalls of the second-hand booksellers (bouquinistes) on the quays of the Left Bank are a landmark. Pore over old postcards, books, posters, comic books and sheet music.

3. Musée d'Orsay Bookshop
As well as its wonderful collections, the museum (p26) has a large and comprehensive art bookshop.

4. YellowKorner La Hune
◻ L4 ◻ 16 Rue de l'Abbaye, 75006
Part gallery, part bookstore, this reincarnation of the St-Germain-des-Prés institution focuses on photography.

5. Boulinier
◻ M4 ◻ 16–18 Blvd St-Michel, 75005
Around in various guises since 1845, Boulinier specializes in second-hand books and magazines, and also CDs, DVDs and vinyl.

6. Album BD
◻ L4 ◻ 8 Rue Dante, 75005
One of several shops on this street selling a wide range of specialist comic books (big business in France) from Tintin to erotica, as well as related merchandise.

7. Librairie Présence Africaine
◻ P6 ◻ 25 bis, Rue des Ecoles, 75005 ◻ Aug
A specialist on books about Africa, as the name suggests. It's an excellent information point, too, if you want to find out where to eat African food or hear African music.

8. San Francisco Book Co.
◻ M5 ◻ 17 Rue Monsieur le Prince, 75006
This hodgepodge of all genres carries exclusive second-hand English books as well as collectibles and a carefully chosen selection of new titles and classics. If you have books to sell, there is usually a buyer on duty.

9. The Red Wheelbarrow
◻ N5 ◻ 9 & 11 Rue de Médicis, 75006
An intimate haven for bibliophiles, French- and English-language books here range from contemporary literature to gastronomy.

10. Abbey Bookshop
◻ N5 ◻ 29 Rue de la Parcheminerie, 75005
This quirky, Canadian-owned shop in the Latin Quarter exudes an aura of timeless, old-world charm and stocks books in French and English. It also serves delicious coffee with maple syrup.

Specialist Food Shops

1. Patrick Roger
F5 **108 Blvd St-Germain, 75006**
One of the new generation of *chocolatiers*, Patrick Roger has already amassed legions of fans thanks to his lifelike sculptures and ganache-filled chocolates.

2. Maison Le Roux
L4 **1 Rue de Bourbon le Château, 75006** **Aug**
The award-winning *chocolatier* offers his trademark salted butter caramels as well as other delicacies such as cacao marshmallows.

3. Jean-Paul Hévin
E6 **3 Rue Vavin, 75006** **Sun, Mon, Aug**
Another distinguished *chocolatier* with elegant, minimalist presentation and superb flavour combinations.

4. Poilâne
E5 **8 Rue du Cherche-Midi, 75006** **Sun**
Founded in the 1930s, this tiny, delicious-smelling bakery produces rustic, naturally leavened loaves in a wood-fired oven.

5. La Dernière Goutte
E5 **6 Rue de Bourbon le Château, 75006**
The English-speaking owners of this wine shop, which specializes in bottles from small producers, also run the nearby wine bar Fish La Boissonnerie.

6. Pierre Hermé
L5 **72 Rue Bonaparte, 75006**
This boutique sells some of the city's finest cakes and pastries, including innovative flavoured macarons.

7. Sadaharu Aoki
E5 **35 Rue de Vaugirard, 75006** **Mon**
Aoki cleverly incorporates Japanese flavours such as yuzu, green tea and black sesame into intoxicating classic French pastries that taste as good as they look.

8. Ryst Dupeyron
N5 **79 Rue du Bac, 75007** **Sun, Mon (am)**
The atmospheric Ryst Dupeyron wine shop, founded in 1905, specializes in fine Bordeaux, rare spirits and vintage Champagne.

9. Barthélémy
J4 **51 Rue de Grenelle, 75007** **Sun & Mon**
Gorgeous farmhouse cheeses are piled high in this charming neighbourhood *fromagerie*.

10. Debauve & Gallais
K4 **30 Rue des Sts-Pères, 75007** **Sun**
This exquisite shop dates from 1800, when chocolate was sold for medicinal purposes.

A range of artisan chocolates at Maison Le Roux

Late-Night Bars

1. Café de la Mairie
K5 **8 Pl St-Sulpice, 75006**
This is an old-fashioned Parisian café, which offers great views of Église St-Sulpice from its busy pavement terrace. It is open until 2am daily except Sunday.

2. Prescription Cocktail Club
L4 **23 Rue Mazarine, 75006**
The expertly mixed drinks are the main attraction at this chic and hip cocktail bar.

3. Le Comptoir des Canettes – Chez Georges
E5 **11 Rue des Canettes, 75006**
Night owls flock to this old-school bar, which has been serving cheap beer and wine since 1952. The vaulted basement holds parties until 2am.

4. Castor Club
M4 **14 Rue Hautefeuille, 75006**
Sun & Mon
A clandestine cocktail bar with a great menu and a downstairs floor.

5. Le 10 Bar International
L5 **10 Rue de l'Odéon, 75006**
This atmospheric sangria bar, with an old jukebox, has been a neighbourhood institution since 1955. Happy hour is 6–8pm.

Well-stocked bar at The Bombardier, known for its British fare

6. The Bombardier
F5 **2 Pl du Panthéon, 75005**
Sip drinks until late at this *franglais* pub, which offers great views of the Panthéon.

7. Compagnie des Vins Surnaturels
E5 **7 Rue Lobineau, 75006**
This cosy, candlelit bar has a superb wine list that features several thousand wines. Enjoy a glass with a selection of delicious small plates.

8. Le Piano Vache
N6 **8 Rue Laplace, 75005**
Popular with a young crowd, this relaxed, trendy bar, with walls covered in posters, has themed nights dedicated to jazz, rock, punk and pop.

9. Le Bar du Marché
E5 **75 Rue de Seine, 75006**
This corner bar, with a popular terrace, appeals to locals and tourists alike, mostly due to its reasonably priced drinks and jovial waitstaff.

10. O'Neil
E5 **20 Rue des Canettes, 75006**
Artisanal beers, from light, bubbly blondes to thick brown ales, are made on the premises of this pub. Don't forget to tuck in to sweet and savoury *flammekuechen* (Alsatian cream-topped pizza), served until midnight.

Patrons at the picturesque terraced Café de la Mairie

Literary Haunts

1. La Palette
L4 43 Rue de Seine, 75006
 8am–2am daily

This café has been requented by the likes of Henry Miller, Apollinaire and Jacques Prévert.

2. Les Deux Magots
K4 6 Pl St-Germain-des-Prés, 75006 7:30am–1am daily
 lesdeuxmagots.fr

This was home to the literary and artistic élite of Paris, such as Albert Camus and Picasso.

3. Café de Flore
K4 172 Blvd St-Germain, 75006 7:30–1:30am daily
 cafedeflore.fr

Guillaume Apollinaire founded his literary magazine, *Les Soirées de Paris,* here in 1913.

4. Le Procope
L4 13 Rue de l'Ancienne Comédie, 75006 Noon–midnight daily

Dating from the 17th-century, this historic spot is known for its mouth-watering French cuisine, including coq au vin and millefeuille.

5. Le Select
E6 99 Blvd du Montparnasse, 75006 7am–2am daily (to 3am Fri & Sat)

F Scott Fitzgerald and Truman Capote are among many American writers who have drunk in this café.

6. Hotel Pont Royal
J3 5–7 Rue de Montalembert, 75007 11am–11pm daily

Henry Miller drank at the bar here at the time of writing his *Tropic of Capricorn* and *Tropic of Cancer.*

7. Shakespeare and Company
This renowned bookshop *(p136)* was once described by novelist Henry Miller as a "wonderland of books".

Iconic Café de Flore, one of the most celebrated cafés in Paris

8. Brasserie Lipp
L4 151 Blvd St-Germain, 75006 9am–12:45am daily

Ernest Hemingway pays homage to this café in *A Moveable Feast,* and André Gide was also a customer. It sponsors an annual literary prize.

9. La Coupole
E6 102 Blvd du Montparnasse, 75014 8am–midnight daily

This former coal depot became a lavish Art Deco brasserie frequented by Françoise Sagan.

10. Le Petit St-Benoît
K3 4 Rue St-Benoît, 75006 Noon–2:30pm & 6:30–10:30pm Mon–Sat

Albert Camus, Simone de Beauvoir and James Joyce once took their daily coffee here. The ambience is bound to transport you to bygone times.

Picnic Providers

1. Saint Germain Market
📍 L5 🏠 4–6 Rue Lobineau, 75006
🕐 Mon
Find cheeses, charcuterie, foie gras and fresh produce all under one roof in this 19th-century covered market.

2. Judy Market
📍 K6 🏠 18 Rue de Fleurus, 75006
Cold-pressed juices and colourful salads are among the healthy take-away options at this smart canteen.

3. Maubert Market
📍 N5 🏠 Pl Maubert, 75006
This small market specializes in organic produce every Tuesday, Thursday and Saturday morning. A good place to pick up olives, cheese, tomatoes and fruit.

4. Maison Mulot
📍 L4 🏠 76 Rue de Seine, 75006
Tarts, sandwiches and good breads from this upmarket patisserie and deli make for a chic picnic.

5. Naturalia
📍 N6 🏠 36 Rue Monge, 75005
🕐 Sun pm
For a fully organic picnic, look no further than this food shop: breads, wines, cheeses, hams, fruits, desserts and much more.

6. Marché Raspail
📍 J4 🏠 Blvd Raspail, 75006
Superb but pricey produce can be found at this food market held in the morning on Tuesday, Friday and Sunday (when it is all organic).

7. La Rôtisserie d'Argent
📍 P5 🏠 19 Quai de la Tournelle, 75005
Place an advance takeaway order of spit-roasted heritage chicken and other luxe picnic options at this bistro.

8. La Grande Épicerie de Paris
📍 D5 🏠 Le Bon Marché, 38 Rue de Sèvres, 75007
Hunt for treasures such as Breton seaweed butter and *coucou de Rennes* at the food hall in Le Bon Marché (*p73*).

9. Le Pirée
📍 N5 🏠 47 Blvd St-Germain, 75005
Delicious, freshly prepared Greek and Armenian specialities, such as stuffed vegetables and honey-soaked cakes, are sold here.

10. Kayser
📍 P6 🏠 8 Rue Monge, 75005 🕐 Mon
If you don't want to make up your own picnic then try a ready-made sandwich from this bakery. Mouthwatering combinations include goat's cheese with pear.

Stalls at the Saint Germain covered market

Places to Eat

The richly decorated Lapérouse, an 18th-century restaurant

1. Dupin

🚇 J5 🏠 11 Rue Dupin, 75006 🕒 Sun & Mon 🌐 restaurantdupin.com · €€€

Dishes such as scallops and wild mushrooms or confit aubergine are sublime – reserve a table in advance.

2. Baieta

🚇 P5 🏠 5 Rue de Pontoise, 75005 🕒 Sun, Mon 🌐 restaurant-baieta-paris.fr · €€€

Michelin-starred Niçoise chef Julia Sedefdjian cooks with verve at her friendly, stylish bistro. Don't miss the excellent bouillabaisse.

3. Clover Green

🚇 E4 🏠 5 Rue Perronnet, 75007 🕒 Sun, Mon 🌐 jeanfrançoispiege.com/infos-clover-saint-germain · €€

Jean-François Piège's inventive modern cuisine focuses on vegetables and is served in this minimalist cosy bistro with an open kitchen.

4. Le Comptoir du Relais

🚇 L5 🏠 9 Carrefour de l'Odéon, 75006 🌐 hotel-paris-relais-saint-germain.com/restaurant-le-comptoir · €€

Yves Camdeborde's much-praised restaurant, famous for its delicious traditional French cuisine, serves bistro lunches and *prix fixe* dinners.

5. Lapérouse

🚇 M4 🏠 51 Quai des Grands Augustins, 75006 🕒 Sun 🌐 laperouse.com · €€€

Classic French cuisine is served in a setting that has remained unchanged since 1766.

6. La Crèmerie

🚇 L5 🏠 9 Rue des Quatre Vents, 75006 ☎ 01 43 54 99 30 🕒 Sun · €€

Chef Tsuyoshi Yamakawa creates new interpretations of French classics.

7. La Tour d'Argent

🚇 P5 🏠 15 Quai de la Tournelle, 75005 🕒 Sun, Mon, Aug 🌐 tourdargent.com · €€€

This historic restaurant with fine views of Notre-Dame serves duckling as its speciality.

8. L'Atelier de Joël Robuchon

🚇 E4 🏠 5 Rue de Montalembert, 75007 🌐 atelier-robuchon-saint-germain.com · €€€

Sample mouthwatering French cuisine by Joël Robuchon at this atelier.

9. Les Papilles

🚇 F6 🏠 30 Rue Gay Lussac, 75005 🕒 Sun, Mon, Aug, 25 Dec–1 Jan 🌐 lespapillesparis.fr · €€

Choose your wine straight off the shelves to accompany the great-value menus.

10. Au Moulin à Vent

🚇 P6 🏠 20 Rue des Fossés St-Bernard, 75005 🕒 Sun & Mon 🌐 au-moulinavent.com · €€€

One of the best bistros in Paris. Try the frog legs sautéed in garlic.

JARDIN DES PLANTES

Named after the blooming medicinal herb garden that blankets its eastern side, this quarter is one of the most peaceful areas of Paris. It's also known for a number of historical sights, from the Arènes de Lutèce's well-preserved Roman amphitheatre to the Rue Mouffetard, a lively cobbled street that dates from medieval times. The area is home to a sizable Muslim community, focused on the Grande Mosquée de Paris and the Institut du Monde Arabe cultural centre.

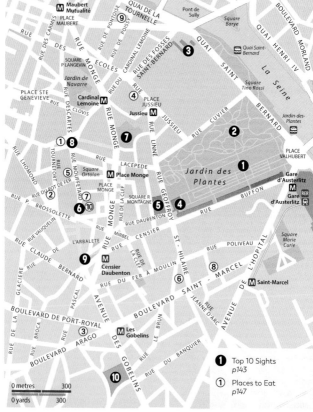

1 Top 10 Sights p143
1 Places to Eat p147

For places to stay in this area, see p178

Beautiful flowers line a path of the Jardin des Plantes

1 Jardin des Plantes

📍 G6 🏠 57 Rue Cuvier, 75005
🕐 8am–8pm daily (to 5:30pm in winter) 🌐 jardindesplantesdeparis.fr

The 17th-century royal medicinal herb garden (*p60*) was planted by two physicians to Louis XIII. Opened in 1640, it flourished under the curatorship of Comte de Buffon and contains thousands of different types of plants. There's a Cedar of Lebanon, planted in 1734, a hillside maze and Alpine gardens.

2 Ménagerie

📍 G6 🏠 Jardin des Plantes, 75005
🕐 Summer: 10am–6pm daily (to 6:30pm Sun & hols); winter: 9am–5pm daily (to 5:30pm Sun & hols) 🌐 jardindesplantesdeparis.fr 🏪

The country's oldest public zoo was founded during the Revolution to house the surviving animals from the royal menagerie at Versailles. Other animals were donated from circuses around the world. However, during the Siege of Paris in 1870–71, most of the unfortunate creatures were eaten by hungry citizens. The zoo is a big favourite with children, and feeding times are especially popular.

3 Institut du Monde Arabe

📍 G5 🏠 1 Rue des Fossés St-Bernard, Pl Mohammed V, 75005
🕐 10am–6pm Tue–Fri, 10am–7pm Sat & Sun 🌐 imarabe.org 🏪

This institute was founded in 1980 to promote cultural relations between France and the Arab world. The stunning building (1987) designed by architect Jean Nouvel features a southern wall of 240 ornate photo-sensitive metal screens that open and close like camera apertures to regulate light entering the building. The design is based on the traditional latticed wooden screens of Islamic architecture. Inside is a museum featuring Islamic artworks, from 9th-century ceramics to contemporary art, as well as a shop, tea salon and restaurant.

4 Muséum National d'Histoire Naturelle

📍 G6 🏠 Jardin des Plantes, 75005
🕐 10am–6pm Wed–Mon 🚫 1 Jan, 1 May, 25 Dec 🌐 mnhn.fr 🏪

The Jardin des Plantes houses varied natural history exhibition galleries. The best is the Grande Galerie de l'Evolution (*p64*) which has taxidermied African mammals, a whale skeleton and an endangered species exhibit.

Skull of a T-rex in the Muséum National d'Histoire Naturelle

Diners having lunch at an outdoor café on Rue Mouffetard

5 Grande Mosquée de Paris

G6 2 bis Pl du Puits de l'Ermite, 75005 9am–6pm Sat–Thu Islamic hols grandemosquee deparis.fr

Built in 1922–6, this mosque is the spiritual centre for Parisian Muslims (p53). The Moorish decoration, especially the grand patio, was inspired by the Alhambra in Spain. The minaret soars to nearly 33 m (100 ft). The complex has an Islamic school, tearoom and a hammam reminiscent of North Africa. Book a guided tour to learn more about the place and its significance.

6 Rue Mouffetard

F6

Although Rue Mouffetard is most famous today for its lively street market held every Tuesday to Sunday (p73), it has an equally colourful past. In Roman times this was the main road from Paris to Rome. Some say its name comes from the French word *mouffette* (skunk), as a reference to the odorous River Bièvre (now covered over) where waste was dumped by tanners and weavers from the nearby Gobelins tapestry factory. Though no longer poor nor bohemian, the neighbourhood still has lots of character, with its 17th-century mansard roofs, old-fashioned painted shop signs and affordable restaurants. In the market you can buy everything from Auvergne sausage to horsemeat and perfectly ripened cheeses.

7 Arènes de Lutèce

G6 49 Rue Monge, 75005 Summer: 9am–8:30pm daily; winter: 8am–6pm daily

The remains of the 2nd-century Roman amphitheatre from the settlement of Lutetia (p8) lay buried for centuries and were only discovered in 1869 during construction of Rue Monge. The novelist Victor Hugo, concerned with the preservation of his city's historic buildings, including Notre-Dame (p30), led the campaign for its restoration. The original arena would have had 35 tiers and could seat 15,000 spectators for theatrical performances and gladiator fights.

FRENCH NORTH AFRICA

France has long had close connections with North Africa, though not always harmonious. Its annexation of Algeria in 1834 led to the long and bloody Algerian War of Liberation (1954–62). Relations with Tunisia, which it governed from 1883 to 1956, and Morocco, also granted independence in 1956, were better. Many North Africans now live in Paris.

8 Place de la Contrescarpe

🔲 F5

This bustling square has a village community feel, with busy cafés and restaurants and groups of students from the nearby Lycée Henri-IV hanging out here after dark. In medieval times, it lay outside the city walls, a remnant of which still stands on Rue Clovis. Notice the memorial plaque above the butcher's at No 1, which marks the site of the old Pine Cone Club, a café where François Rabelais and other writers gathered in the 16th century.

9 St-Médard

🔲 G6 🔲 141 Rue Mouffetard, 75005 🕒 9am–7:30pm Tue–Sun (to 8pm Sun) 🌐 saintmedard.org

The church at the bottom of Rue Mouffetard dates back to the 9th century, when it was a parish church dedicated to St Médard, counsellor to the Merovingian kings. The present church, completed in 1655, is a mixture of Flamboyant Gothic and Renaissance styles. Among the fine paintings inside is the 17th-century *St Joseph Walking with the Christ Child* by Francisco de Zurbarán. The churchyard became notorious as it was the scene of hysterical fits in the 18th century, when a cult of *convulsionnaires* sought miracle cures at the grave of a Jansenist deacon.

10 La Manufacture des Gobelins

🔲 42 Ave des Gobelins, 75013 🕒 11am–6pm Tue–Sun 🌐 cultival.fr 🔲

This world-renowned tapestry factory was originally a dyeing workshop, founded by the Gobelin brothers in the mid-15th century. In 1662, Louis XIV's minister Colbert set up a royal factory here and gathered the greatest craftsmen of the day to make furnishings for the palace at Versailles *(p159)*. Visitors can observe the traditional weaving process on a guided tour, which usually takes place on Wednesday afternoons. Make sure to book ahead.

A DAY IN THE GARDENS

Morning

Start the day around 8am by browsing the stalls at the market on **Rue Mouffetard**. Working upwards from the bottom of the street and the church of **St-Médard**, you'll find plenty here to make up a delicious breakfast, whether from the many market stalls or from the grocers and cafés that dot the street. Splendid old buildings mark this medieval street.

Follow Rue Mouffetard up to the café-lined **Place de la Contrescarpe**, then head to the **Grande Galerie de l'Evolution** *(p143)*, one of several natural history galleries to be found in the **Jardin des Plantes** *(p143)*. Stroll through the **gardens** and take a break on a bench to admire the flowerbeds. Exit through the gate on Rue Cuvier, near Rue Linné, and make a detour to the **Arènes de Lutèce** on your way to **Le Buisson Ardent** *(p147)* for a simple, authentic bistro lunch.

Afternoon

Spend part of the afternoon at **the Institut du Monde Arabe** *(p143)*, exploring its beautiful Islamic artworks, before walking down to admire the Moorish architecture of the **Grande Mosquée de Paris**. End the day with a mint tea and a selection of maamoul and baklava at the **Café-Restaurant de la Mosquée** *(39 Rue Geoffroy St-Hilaire; open noon–midnight daily)*.

Jardin des Plantes Sights

Entrance to the Grandes Serres in the Jardin des Plantes

1. Dinosaur Tree
One of the trees in the Botanical Gardens is a *Ginkgo biloba*, which was planted in 1795, but the species is known to have existed in exactly the same form in the days of the dinosaurs, 125 million years ago.

2. Cedar of Lebanon
This magnificent tree was planted in 1734 and came from London's Botanic Gardens in Kew, although a story grew up that its seed was brought here all the way from Syria in the hat of a scientist.

3. Rose Garden
Having only been planted in 1990 and so relatively modern compared to the other gardens, the beautiful *roseraie* has nearly 350 varieties of roses and 180 rose bushes on display. It is spectacular when in full bloom in spring and summer.

4. Rock Gardens
One of the stars of the Botanical Gardens, with more than 2,000 plants from the world's diverse Alpine regions. There are samples from Corsica to the Caucasus, Morocco and the Himalayas.

5. Sophora Japonica
Sent to Paris under the label "unknown Chinese tree" by a Jesuit naturalist living in China, this tree, often called a Pagoda Tree, was planted in 1747, first flowered in 1777, and still flowers today.

6. Iris Garden
An unusual feature is this designated garden which brings together more than 100 different varieties of irises.

7. Dodo Manège
The strange and exotic animals on this magical merry-go-round (*p65*) include a dodo, a triceratops, a horned turtle and even a sivatherium, a giraffe-like animal with antlers.

8. Nile Crocodile
The crocodile in the Reptile House now has a better home than he once did. He was found in 1998, when he was six months old, in the bathtub of a Paris hotel room, left behind as an unwanted pet.

9. Young Animal House
One of the zoo's most popular features for children is this house where young creatures, which for one reason or another cannot be looked after by their natural parents, are raised. Once they have reached adulthood they are returned to their natural habitat.

10. Greenhouses
One of the best things about the gardens are the huge Grandes Serres. One of the 19th-century greenhouses charts the evolution of plants, while the other is home to a range of flora from New Caledonia. A later Art Deco-style glasshouse is dedicated to a variety of tropical rainforest plants.

Places to Eat

1. DOSE – Dealer de Café
📍 F6 🏠 73 Rue Mouffetard, 75005
🗓 Mon 🌐 la-truffiere.fr · €
Some of the best espresso and cappuccinos in Paris are served at this coffee shop. It also offers delicious healthy salads and toasties.

2. Chez Léna et Mimile
📍 F6 🏠 32 Rue Tournefort, 75005 🗓 Sun & Mon 🌐 chezlenaetmimile.fr · €€
Grab lunch or dinner at this charming family-run bistro on quiet little Rue Tournefort. The peaceful terrace is an undoubted highlight.

3. Au Petit Marguery
📍 F6 🏠 9 Blvd de Port-Royal, 75013
🌐 petitmarguery-rivegauche.fr · €€
One for meat lovers, with steak, veal and game on the menu. Also try the Grand Marnier soufflé, a house speciality.

4. Le Buisson Ardent
📍 G6 🏠 25 Rue Jussieu, 75005
📞 01 43 54 93 02 🗓 Sun · €€
This bistro is a romantic nighttime destination serving French dishes with a twist. Set menus offer good value.

5. Le Vieux Bistrot
📍 F6 🏠 54 Rue Mouffetard, 75005
🗓 Tue 🌐 levieuxbistrot-paris.fr · €€
A charming family-style French bistro, complete with checkered tablecloths, that specializes in fondue and raclettes.

6. L'Agrume
📍 G6 🏠 15 Rue des Fossés St-Marcel, 75005 🗓 Sun & Mon 🌐 restaurant-lagrume.fr · €€€
Seafood fresh from Brittany features on the menu at this popular bistro. There are good-value set lunches too.

7. La Truffière
📍 F6 🏠 4 Rue Blainville, 75005
🗓 Sun & Mon 🌐 dose.paris · €€€
A 17th-century building, a wood fire and welcoming staff all make for a great little Michelin-approved bistro. Naturally, the menu features delectable truffles.

8. Au Coco de Mer
📍 G6 🏠 34 Blvd St-Marcel, 75005
🗓 Sun D, Mon L 🌐 cocodemer.fr · €€
This restaurant serves spicy Seychelles cuisine, usually including vegetarian options, and has a "beach hut" terrace with soft sand.

9. Kitchen Ter(re)
📍 G5 🏠 26 Blvd St-Germain, 75005
🗓 Sun & Mon 🌐 zehitchengalerie.fr · €€
Italian and Asian flavours mix at chef William Ledeuil's zesty restaurant, which specializes in homemade pasta.

10. Flocon
📍 F6 🏠 75 Rue Mouffetard, 75005
🗓 Mon & Tue 🌐 restaurantflocon.com · €€
Locals applauded the opening of this well-priced bistro, where the imaginative cooking might include dishes such as artichoke carpaccio and buttery skate.

Le Buisson Ardent, an old-fashioned brasserie with a street terrace

The spectacular main gallery in the Muséum National d'Histoire Naturelle

MONTMARTRE AND PIGALLE

With its cobbled streets and charming houses, Montmartre manages to retain the feel of a 19th-century village in the middle of Paris. The area was a hub for painters and poets in the 19th and early 20th centuries. Today, visitors come to explore the Sacré-Coeur basilica. Slightly grittier, the neighbouring Pigalle, once home to dance halls and cabarets, is now better known for its adult shows and nightlife.

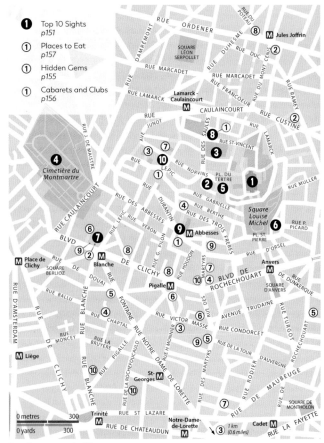

1 **Top 10 Sights**
 p151

① **Places to Eat**
 p157

① **Hidden Gems**
 p155

① **Cabarets and Clubs**
 p156

For places to stay in this area, see p178

Cimetière de Montmartre, the final resting place for many luminaries

1 Sacré-Coeur

One of the city's most photographed sights, the basilica of Sacré-Coeur *(p36)*, dedicated to the Sacred Heart of Christ, watches over Paris from on high.

2 Dalí Paris

F1 ⬛ 11 Rue Poulbot, 75018
🕐 10am–6pm daily ⬛ daliparis. com ⬛

The Dalí works here may not be the artist's most famous, but this museum is still a must-visit for any fan of the Spanish Surrealist. The impressive private collection – France's largest – of Dalí's paintings, sculptures, engravings, objects and furniture reveals the dramatic character of the 20th-century Catalan genius. Look out for the bronzes of his memorable "fluid" clocks.

3 Musée de Montmartre

⬛ 12 Rue Cortot, 75018
🕐 10am–6pm daily ⬛ museede montmartre.fr ⬛

The museum is set in Montmartre's finest townhouse, known as Le Manoir de Rosimond after the 17th-century actor who once owned it. From 1875 it provided living quarters and studios for numerous artists, including Suzanne Valadon and her son Maurice Utrillo; her studio and apartment have been restored and form part of the museum. Using drawings, photos and other memorabilia, the museum presents the history of Montmartre, from its 12th-century convent days to the present, with an emphasis on the free-spirited lifestyle of the belle époque. There is even a recreated 19th-century bistro, as well as gardens where Renoir painted.

4 Cimetière de Montmartre

⬛ E1 ⬛ 20 Ave Rachel, 75018
⬛ paris.fr

The main graveyard for the district lies beneath a busy road in an old gypsum quarry, though it's more restful than it first appears once you actually get below street level. The illustrious tombs, many with ornately sculpted monuments, packed tightly into this intimate space, reflect the artistic bent of the residents, who include composers Offenbach and Berlioz, writers Stendhal and Dumas, Russian dancer Nijinsky as well as the iconic film director François Truffaut.

5 Place du Tertre

⬛ F1

At 130 m (430 ft), Montmartre's old village square, whose name means "hillock", is the highest point in the city. Nearby is the church of St-Pierre de Montmartre, all that remains of the Benedictine abbey which stood here from 1133 until the Revolution.

Portrait artist in the Place du Tertre

6 Halle Saint Pierre

⬛ F1 ⬛ 2 Rue Ronsard, 75018
⬛ 11am–6pm Mon–Fri, 11am–7pm
Sat, noon–6pm Sun ⬛ Public
hols, weekends in Aug ⬛ hallesaint
pierre.org ⬛

The former covered market is
now a cultural centre, which hosts
temporary exhibitions of Art Brut.
Coined by the painter Jean Dubuffet
in 1945, the concept of Art Brut
encompasses works created outside
the boundaries of "official" culture,
often by psychiatric patients, prisoners
and children. The centre also has a
permanent collection of native folk
art. It stages avant-garde theatre
and musical productions and holds
literary evenings and debates.

**Pretty exterior of Au Lapin Agile,
a rustic restaurant and cabaret**

7 Moulin Rouge

⬛ E1 ⬛ 82 Blvd de Clichy, 75018
⬛ Shows at 9pm & 11pm daily
(dinner: 7pm) ⬛ moulinrouge.fr

The Moulin Rouge ("red windmill")
is the most famous of the belle
époque dance halls that once scan-
dalized respectable citizens and
attracted Montmartre's artists and
other colourful characters. Henri de
Toulouse-Lautrec immortalized the
era with his sketches and posters of
dancers such as Jane Avril, some of which
now grace the Musée d'Orsay (p26).
Cabaret shows are still performed here.

8 Au Lapin Agile

⬛ F1 ⬛ 22 Rue des Saules,
75018 ⬛ 9pm–1am Tue–Sun
⬛ au-lapin-agile.com

This belle époque restaurant and
cabaret (p156) is a landmark venue in
a 19th-century stone house. It was a
popular hangout for Picasso and
Renoir, and poets Apollinaire and
Paul Verlaine. It took its name from
a humorous painting by André Gill
of a rabbit (lapin) leaping out of a
cooking pot, called the Lapin à Gill.
In time it became known by its
current name ("nimble rabbit").

THE MONTMARTRE VINEYARDS

It's hard to imagine it today, but Montmartre was once a French wine region said to match the quality of Bordeaux and Burgundy. There were 20,000 ha (50,000 acres) of Parisian vineyards in the mid-18th century, but today just 1,500 bottles of wine are made annually from the remaining 2,000 vines in Montmartre, and are sold in aid of charity.

9 Place des Abbesses
□ E1

This pretty square lies at the base of the Butte Montmartre. Visit it via the metro station of the same name to appreciate one of the few original Art Nouveau stations left in the city. Designed by the architect Hector Guimard in 1900, it features green wrought-iron arches, amber lanterns and a ship shield, the symbol of Paris. Along with Porte Dauphine, it is the only station entrance to retain its original glass roof. A mural painted by local artists winds around the spiral stair-case at the entrance. But don't walk to the platform, take the lift – it's the deepest station in Paris, with 285 steps.

10 Moulin de la Galette
□ E1 □ 83 Rue Lepic, 75018
□ moulindelagaletteparis.com

Montmartre once had more than 30 windmills, used for pressing grapes and grinding wheat; this is one of only two still standing. During the siege of Paris in 1814 its owner, Pierre-Charles Debray, was crucified on its sails by Russian soldiers. It became a dance hall in the 19th century and inspired paintings by Renoir and Van Gogh (p27). Another windmill on the same street, the Moulin Radet, houses a restaurant confusingly also called Le Moulin de la Galette.

**The revue show "Féerie"
on the stage of Moulin Rouge**

A DAY IN MONTMARTRE

Morning

The sooner you get to **Sacré-Coeur** (p36) the more you will have it to yourself – it opens at 6am. Later in the morning, enjoy the bustle of Montmartre, and watch tourists having their portraits painted by the area's street artists in the **Place du Tertre** (p151). There are plenty of coffee places to choose from, but the one most of the artists frequent is the **Clairon des Chasseurs** (3 Pl du Tertre; open 7am–2am daily).

For art of a more surreal kind, visit **Dalí Paris** (p151). Head down Rue des Saules to continue the artistic theme with lunch at **La Maison Rose** (2 Rue de l'Abreuvoir). Utrillo once painted this pink restaurant.

Afternoon

Musée de Montmartre (p151) is close by, as are the Montmartre Vineyards, and also the little **Cimetière de St-Vincent** where you will find Maurice Utrillo's grave.

Walk back up to Rue Lepic, which is a great place to shop. Next, see the **Moulin de la Galette** before heading towards the **Place des Abbesses**, one of Paris's most picturesque squares. Don't miss the famous entrance to the Art Nouveau metro station.

To the south is a great bar for an aperitif, **La Fourmi** (74 Rue des Martyrs). Then finish the day in style with a show at the **Moulin Rouge** cabaret.

Artists who Lived in Montmartre

Reclining Nude (1928) by Suzanne Valadon, an oil painting

1. Suzanne Valadon
Suzanne Valadon (1865–1938) was one of the first female painters to find success in Montmartre. Today her bold masterpieces, challenging the conventions of the nude, are displayed in France and even at the Met in New York.

2. Salvador Dalí
The Catalan painter (1904–89) came to Paris in 1929 and held his first Surrealist exhibition that year. He kept a studio in Montmartre, and his work is now celebrated in Dalí Paris (p151).

3. Vincent van Gogh
The Dutch artist (1853–90) lived for a time on the third floor of 54 Rue Lepic. His early paintings were inspired by the Moulin de la Galette windmill (p153).

4. Edgar Degas
The French artist Edgar Degas was born in Paris in 1834 and lived in the city for the whole of his life, most of the time in Montmartre, painting many of its street scenes and characters. He died here in 1917 and is buried in Montmartre cemetery (p151).

5. Louise Weber
Popularly known as La Goulue, Weber (1866-1929) was a well-known dancer at the Moulin Rouge, famous for her performances of the traditional cancan. Her fall from fame was almost as talked about as her rise to stardom.

6. Maurice Utrillo
Maurice Utrillo (1883–1955) lived with his artist mother, Suzanne Valadon, at 12 Rue Cortot, now the Musée de Montmartre (p151). His painted cityscapes include many atmospheric depictions of old Montmartre.

7. Henri de Toulouse-Lautrec
More than any other artist, Toulouse-Lautrec (1864–1901) is associated with Montmartre for his sketches and posters of dancers at the Moulin Rouge and other dance halls. For most people, they epitomize the era to this day.

8. Dalida
France's disco queen, Dalida (1933–87) performed over 700 songs in several languages, which are still popular today.

9. Amedeo Modigliani
The Italian painter and sculptor (1884–1920) arrived in Paris in 1906, when he was 22, and was greatly influenced by Toulouse-Lautrec and the other famous bohemian artists on the Montmartre scene.

10. Pierre-Auguste Renoir
Renoir (1841–1919) is another artist who found inspiration in the Moulin de la Galette, when he lived at 12 Rue Cortot. For a time he laid tables at Au Lapin Agile (p152).

Portrait of French painter and sculptor, Edgar Degas

Hidden Gems

1. St-Jean-l'Évangéliste de Montmartre

⚐ E1 **⌂** 19 Rue des Abbesses, 75018
This 1904 church is a clash of styles, from Moorish to Art Nouveau.

2. 18th-Arrondissement City Hall

⌂ 1 Pl Jules Joffrin, 75018
On display in this building are two Utrillo paintings.

3. Hameau des Artistes

⚐ E1 **⌂** 11 Ave Junot, 75018
This little hamlet of artists' studios is private, but no one will mind if you take a quiet look around.

4. Musée de la Vie Romantique

⚐ E1 **⌂** 16 Rue Chaptal, 75009
⌚ 10am–6pm Tue–Sun **♿**
George Sand was a frequent visitor to this chamring house, which is now devoted to the writer.

5. Rue des Martyrs

⚐ E1
Filled with food shops and cafés, this hilly street leading up to Montmartre is mostly full of locals and travellers looking for a reprieve.

6. Cité Véron

⚐ E1 **⌂** 92 Blvd de Clichy, 75018
This bucolic cul-de-sac is home to the Académie des Arts Chorégraphiques, a prestigious dance school.

7. Square Suzanne Buisson

⚐ E1
Named after a World War II Resistance fighter, this square is a quiet spot to unwind and relax.

8. Rue du Poteau

A great market street with an authentic local feel.

9. Crypte du Martyrium de St-Denis

⚐ E1 **⌂** 11 Rue Yvonne Le Tac, 75018
⌚ 3–6pm Fri, 1st Sat & Sun of the month **🌐** cryptemartyrium-paris.cef.fr

A simple 19th-century chapel, this is said to be on the spot where St Denis, the patron saint of France, was beheaded by the Romans in 250 CE.

10. Musée Gustave Moreau

⚐ E2 **⌂** 14 Rue de La Rochefoucauld, 75009 **⌚** 10am–6pm Wed–Mon
🌐 musee-moreau.fr **♿**

The former home of Symbolist artist Moreau displays a large collection of his imaginative works.

Fantastic spiral staircase in the Musée Gustave Moreau

Cabarets and Clubs

1. Au Lapin Agile
Poets and artists not only drank in this cabaret club *(p152)*, some – such as Renoir and Verlaine – also laid tables. Picasso even paid his bill with one of his Harlequin paintings.

2. Moulin Rouge
As old as the Eiffel Tower (1889) and as much a part of the Parisian image, today's troupe of 60 Doriss Girls are the modern versions of Jane Avril and La Goulue. Since its establishment, Moulin Rouge has become synonymous with the energetic dance style known as the French cancan.

3. Silencio
🅿 F3 🏠 142 Rue Montmartre, 75002
Ⓦ lesilencio.com
David Lynch's club, which opens to the general public from 11pm, mixes art, theatre and music in one of Paris's most eclectic nightlife venues.

4. La Cantine de la Cigale
🅿 E1 🏠 124 Blvd Marguerite de Rochechouart, 75018
📞 01 55 79 10 10
A popular brasserie by day, this lively hangout, next to the famed La Cigale theatre, hosts DJ sets on Friday and Saturday nights.

5. La Nouvelle Eve
🅿 E1 🏠 25 Rue Pierre Fontaine, 75009
Ⓦ lanouvelleeveparis.com
One of the lesser-known cabaret venues produces professional shows that feature colourful displays of the celebrated French cancan.

6. Lulu White
🅿 E1 🏠 12 Rue Frochot, 75009
🕐 Sun Ⓦ luluwhite.bar
One of many cocktail bars springing up in South Pigalle, this one serves absinthe-based drinks and hosts jazz.

Red façade of Moulin Rouge, an iconic symbol of Parisian nightlife

7. Cabaret Michou
🅿 E1 🏠 80 Rue des Martyrs, 75018
Ⓦ michou.com
With outrageous drag artists and a compère whose behaviour can never be predicted, this place is close to the original spirit of Montmartre cabaret.

8. Les Trois Baudets
🅿 E1 🏠 64 Blvd de Clichy, 75018
Ⓦ lestroisbaudets.com
Famous French singer Serge Gainsbourg got his start at this venue.

9. La Machine du Moulin Rouge
🅿 E1 🏠 90 Blvd de Clichy, 75018
Ⓦ lamachinedumoulinrouge.com
Next to the Moulin Rouge, this venue hosts both club nights and concerts.

10. Le Divan du Monde
🅿 E1 🏠 75 Rue des Martyrs, 75018
Ⓦ divandumonde.com 🔗
World music gigs and a drag cabaret act coexist at this quirky spot.

Places to Eat

1. Le Coq & Fils
⚑ E1 ⌂ 98 Rue Lepic, 75018
ⓦ lecoq-fils.com · €€
Poultry is the star of the show at chef
Antoine Westermann's bistro. Try the
rotisserie-style Bresse chicken.

2. Meha
⌂ 35 Rue Ramey, 75018 ⓦ meha.paris
· €
A neighbourhood restaurant serving
affordable, bistro-style gastronomy with
French, Japanese and Moroccan influ-
ences. Expect dishes like braised veal
cheeks, gambas ravioli and baba rhum.

3. Buvette
⚑ E1 ⌂ 28 Rue Henry Monnier, 75009
ⓦ ilovebuvette.com · €
Under a gorgeous tin ceiling, this
comfortable New York-style bistro
serves cocktails, a mouthwatering
chocolate mousse and classic French
dishes prepared using locally sourced
ingredients. Linger over a hearty
brunch at the weekend.

4. Le Relais de la Butte
⚑ E1 ⌂ 12 Rue Ravignan, 75018
ⓦ lerelaisdelabutte.fr · €
A pavement café (p71) perfect
for sipping coffee, tucking into a
charcuterie board or indulging
in a glass of wine.

**Trendy Buvette, with its tin
ceiling and well-stocked bar**

5. Pétrelle
⚑ F1 ⌂ 34 Rue Pétrelle, 75009 ⏲ Mon,
Tue, Wed–Fri L ⓦ petrelle.fr · €€€
A restaurant with a cosy atmosphere
and a menu using only local produce.

6. Le Pantruche
⚑ F1 ⌂ 3 Rue Victor Massé, 75009 ⏲ Sat
& Sun ⓦ lapantruchoise.com · €€
This bistro is a great go-to for
French classics with fun twists.

7. Restaurant Caillebotte
⚑ F2 ⌂ 8 Rue Hippolyte Lebas, 75009
⏲ Sun ⓦ lapantruchoise.com/
caillebotte · €€
Elegant yet simple dining with a
contemporary edge, tucked away
from Rue des Martyrs.

8. Bouillon Pigalle
⚑ E1 ⌂ 22 Blvd de Clichy, 75018
ⓦ bouillonlesite.com · €
A modern take on the classic French
eatery, Bouillon Pigalle serves well-
priced traditional fare. Reservation
in advance is recommended.

9. Hôtel Amour
⚑ F2 ⌂ 8 Rue de Navarin, 75009
ⓦ hotelamourparis.fr · €€
The modish restaurant in this hip
hotel serves internationally inspired
food with a mix of French classics.

10. Gargouille
⌂ 7 Rue Jean-Baptiste Pigalle
75009 ⏲ Sat & Sun ⓦ gargouille-
restaurant.fr· €€
Mediterranean-influenced sharing
plates and organic wines go down
well at this Art Deco-style bistro.

GREATER PARIS

Central Paris has more than enough on offer to keep
any visitor occupied, but if time permits you should
make at least one foray out of the centre, whether it
be to the sumptuous Palace of Versailles, former home
of the Sun King Louis XIV, or to the Magic Kingdom of
Disneyland® Paris. The excellent metro system makes
for easy day trips to the area's two main parks, the Bois
de Boulogne and the Bois de Vincennes, for a wide range
of outdoor activities, from boating to horse riding, or
just strolling amid pleasant greenery. In contrast to
these bucolic pleasures is the cutting-edge modern
architecture of La Défense. Visually stunning, it com-
prises Paris's high-rise business district, with added
attractions in its exhibition centres. It was launched
in 1958 to create a new home for leading French and
multinational companies. Since then, a major artistic
scheme has transformed several of the squares into
fascinating open-air museums. Two large cemeteries
outside the centre are worth a visit for their ornate tombs.

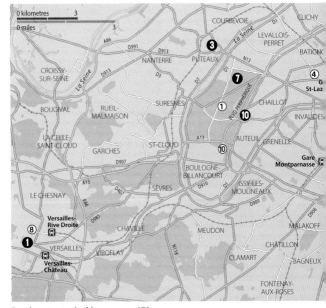

For places to stay in this area, see p179

The opulent Hall of Mirrors at the Palace of Versailles

1 Versailles

📍 Pl d'Armes, 78000 Versailles 🕐 Château: 9am–6:30pm Tue– Sun (Nov–Mar: to 5:30pm); gardens: 8am–8:30pm daily (Nov–Mar: to 6pm) 🕐 Public hols 🌐 chateauversailles.fr 🔗

The top day trip from Paris has to be Versailles. This stunning chateau, begun by Louis XIV around 1662, is overwhelming in its opulence and scale. Plan what you want to see and arrive early, as even a full day may not be long enough. If you'd like to spend a few days exploring, opt for the two-day passport, which includes an equestrian show at the Académie Equestre de Versailles.

2 Disneyland® Paris

📍 Marne-la-Vallée 🕐 Hours vary, chech website 🌐 disneylandparis.com

Since its opening in 1992, this theme park still draws more people than the Louvre and the Eiffel Tower combined. In the shadow of the extravagant Château de la Belle au Bois Dormant (Sleeping Beauty Castle), visitors will enjoy the high-tech workings and imagination behind such attractions as the multisensory 4D Ratatouille ride and the rollicking Pirates of the Caribbean ride. At the adjacent Walt Disney Studios® Park, dedicated to Disney's movies and television shows, you can experience the thrill of special-effects rides and professional stunt shows. Marvel, Star Wars and Frozen attractions are the latest additions to the park.

3 La Défense

🌐 parisladefense.com

French vision and flair coupled with Parisian style are clearly shown by this modern urban development. This business and government centre was purposely built to the west of the city to allow the centre to remain unmarred by skyscrapers. More than just offices, however, the area is also an attraction in its own right, with stunning sights such as the Grande Arche, a cube-like structure with a centre large enough to contain Notre-Dame, and surrounded by artworks, a fountain, cafés and restaurants.

4 Bois de Vincennes

📍 94300 Vincennes 🕐 Park: 24 hours daily; château: 10am–5pm (Jun–Aug: to 6pm) 🚫 Public hols 🌐 chateau-vincennes.fr

Southeast of the city lies the Bois de Vincennes (p60), which has several lakes with boating facilities, beautiful formal gardens at the Parc Floral, the city's main zoo, and play areas. The Château de Vincennes was a royal residence before Versailles and has the tallest keep in Europe. The more energetic can walk here all the way from the Bastille along the Promenade Plantée, which follows, part way, a former railway viaduct.

5 Parc de la Villette

📍 211 Ave Jean-Jaurès, 75019 🕐 Hours vary, check website 🌐 lavillette.com ♿

Once home to slaughterhouses and a livestock market, this former industrial area has been transformed into a vibrant urban park (p64). The landscape was designed by Bernard Tschumi in 1993 to a futuristic design. It provides the usual park features of gardens and playgrounds, but sculptures, zany elements like bright red pavilions and several major attractions offer a different edge. These include the Philharmonie de Paris concert hall and museum; the Cité des Sciences et de l'Industrie, an interactive science museum; and an Omnimax cinema in a geodesic dome. In the summer, the park holds an open-air film festival.

The geodesic dome of La Geode in the Parc de la Villette

Montparnasse Cemetery, the resting place of many illustrious Parisians

6 Montparnasse

🕐 Cemetery: 8am–6pm Mon–Fri, 8:30am–6pm Sat, 9am–6pm Sun (mid-Nov–mid-Mar: to 5:30pm) 🌐 tourmontparnasse56.com

The area of Montparnasse is always recognizable due to the 210-m (689-ft) Tour Montparnasse, which offers spectacular views. Five minutes' walk away is the area's main draw, the Cimetière du Montparnasse, where the great writers Maupassant, Sartre, de Beauvoir, Baudelaire and Samuel Beckett are buried. Nearby, too, the Catacombs (p62) offer an intriguing underground experience of the city.

7 Bois de Boulogne

📍 A2

This enormous park with its 856 ha (2,135 acres) is Parisians' favourite green retreat, especially on summer weekends. Besides the usual walking and picnicking, it also offers cycling, horse riding, boating or visiting the various attractions – including parks within the park, two race courses and the striking Frank Gehry-designed Fondation Louis Vuitton (p163) contemporary arts centre.

8 Canal St-Martin

📍 G2

Completed in 1825, this 4.5-km (2.8-mile) canal was commissioned by Napoleon Bonaparte as a goods supply route for Paris. Today, the canal has become a hot spot for daytime coffee dates and evening picnics, fuelled by the surrounding area's extensive selection of cafés. It's also a great place to cycle or stretch your legs.

9 Cimetière Père Lachaise

📍 Opp 21 boulevard de Ménilmontant, 75020 📞 01 55 25 82 10 🕐 8am–5:30pm Mon–Fri, 8:30am–5:30pm Sat, 9am–5:30pm Sun (Mar–Nov: to 6pm)

This is the most visited cemetery in the world, largely due to rock music fans who come from around the world to see the grave of the legendary singer Jim Morrison of The Doors. There are about one million other graves here, and some 70,000 different tombs, including those of Chopin, Oscar Wilde, Balzac, É dith Piaf, Colette, Molière and Delacroix. There are maps posted around the cemetery to help you find the most famous graves (p164), and it's also possible to download a map from paris.fr/cimetieres.

10 Musée Marmottan Monet

📍 2 Rue Louis-Boilly, 75016 🕐 10am–6pm Tue–Sun (to 9pm Thu) 🌐 marmottan.fr 🔗

Paul Marmottan was an art historian and his 19th-century mansion now houses the world's largest collection of works by Claude Monet, including his *Impression, Soleil Levant*, which gave the Impressionist movement its name.

THE TREATY OF VERSAILLES

France, the UK, the US, Italy and Germany negotiated this agreement after World War I at Versailles, which required Germany to demilitarize parts of its territory, reduce the size of its army, abolish conscription, cease trading in military equipment and pay compensation. The Treaty was signed on 28 June 1919.

A DAY IN THE BOIS DE VINCENNES

Morning

To immerse yourself in greenery, head to the **Bois de Vincennes**. Take metro line 1 to **Château de Vincennes**, stopping off at **Le Drapeau** brasserie *(18 Ave de Paris; open daily)* for a cup of coffee.

Cross the road (or follow signs from the metro if you skipped coffee) to the medieval castle that was at the heart of the French monarchy until 1682, when Louis XIV decided to settle in Versailles. Look out for the ornate gate and stained-glass windows of the Gothic **Sainte-Chapelle** *(p44)*.

For lunch, try **La Table des Troys** *(2 bis Ave de Paris; open daily)*, just opposite the fortress, serving familiar staples of French cuisine.

Afternoon

After lunch take a walk amid the flowers and plants in the **Parc Floral de Paris** *(p63)* within the Bois, then head for the kitsch mini-golf course featuring models of Parisian monuments. Afterwards, stroll to **Lac Daumesnil**, where you can rent a boat to row around the lake's two islands.

From the **Porte Dorée metro** station, near the Art Deco Palais de la Porte Dorée, take the metro west to the Aligre quarter. Get off at **Ledru-Rollin** and walk to the **Baron Rouge** *(p103)* for an aperitif.

Versailles Sights

1. The Hall of Mirrors
The spectacular 70-m- (233-ft-) long Galerie des Glaces has been magnificently restored. It was in this room that the Treaty of Versailles was signed in 1919, formally ending World War I.

2. Chapelle Royale
The Royal Chapel is regarded as one of the finest Baroque buildings in the country. Finished in 1710, its elegant, white marble Corinthian columns and numerous murals make for an awe-inspiring place of prayer.

3. Salon de Venus
In this elaborate room, which is decorated predominantly in marble, a statue of Louis XIV, the creator of Versailles, stands centre stage, exuding regal splendour beneath the fine painted ceiling.

4. Queen's Bedchamber
Nineteen royal infants were born in this opulent room, which has been meticulously restored to exactly how it appeared when it was last used by Marie-Antoinette in 1789.

5. Queen's Hamlet
Behind the Petit Trianon is the Queen's Hamlet, a life-size model village, built for Marie-Antoinette, that was also a functioning farm. The cottages, inspired by rural French architecture, have rustic exteriors, but the interiors are richly furnished.

6. Salon d'Apollon
Louis XIV's throne room is, naturally, one of the palace's centrepieces, and features a suitably regal portrait of the great Sun King. Dedicated to the god Apollo, it strikingly reflects the French monarchy's divine self-image.

7. L'Opéra Royal
The opulent opera house was built in 1770 for the marriage of the Dauphin, the future Louis XVI, to Marie-Antoinette. The floors were designed so that they could be raised to stage level during special festivals.

8. Le Domaine de Trianon
In the southeast corner of the gardens, Louis XIV and Louis XV had the Grand and Petit Trianon palaces built as "private" retreats. Marie-Antoinette was given the Petit Trianon by Louis XVI.

9. Palace Gardens
The palace gardens feature many walkways, landscaped topiary, fountains, pools, statues and the Orangery, where exotic plants were kept in the winter. The magnificent Fountain of Neptune is situated to the north of the North Wing.

10. Royal Stables
These magnificent stables, have been restored and they now house the famous Bartabas Academy of Equestrian Arts.

Stunning ceiling paintings at the Royal Chapel

Rowing boats for hire on a lake at Bois de Boulogne

Bois de Boulogne Features

1. Parc de Bagatelle
Differing garden styles feature in this park, including English and Japanese, though for most visitors the major attraction is the huge rose garden, best seen in June.

2. Jardin du Pré-Catelan
This park-within-a-park is at the very centre of the Bois. Its lawns and wooded areas include a magnificent 200-year-old beech tree and the idyllic eponymous restaurant (p165).

3. Jardin d'Acclimatation
This children's dream of a playpark (p64), dating from 1860 and located within the Bois de Boulogne, has some 45 activities and rides, including a river ride, roller coaster and climbing ropes.

4. La Grande Cascade
This artificial waterfall was a major undertaking when the park was built, requiring concrete to be shipped down the Seine.

5. Lakes
Two long, thin lakes adjoin each other. The larger of the two, confusingly called Lac Inférieur (the other is Lac Supérieur) has boats for hire and a motor boat to take you to the islands.

6. Fondation Louis Vuitton
A thrilling example of modern architecture, this spectacular glass building (p56), designed by Frank Gehry, is a cultural centre dedicated to modern art. It hosts regular art events and exhibitions.

7. Château de Longchamp
While he redesigned central Paris (p10), Baron Haussmann landscaped the Bois de Boulogne. This chateau was given to him by Napoleon III.

8. Shakespeare Garden
In the Jardin du Pré-Catelan is a little garden planted with all the trees, flowers and herbs mentioned in the plays of Shakespeare. There is a lovely open-air theatre.

9. Jardin des Serres d'Auteuil
This 19th-century garden has a series of greenhouses where ornamental hothouse plants are grown. In the centre is a palm house with tropical plants.

10. Horse-Racing
The Bois is home to two race courses. To the west is the Hippodrome de Longchamp, where flat racing takes place, including the Qatar Prix de l'Arc de Triomphe (p77); meanwhile in the east, the Hippodrome d'Auteuil holds steeplechases.

Notable Graves

The gravestone of Édith Piaf in Cimetière du Père-Lachaise

1. Jim Morrison, Cimetière du Père Lachaise

The American lead singer of The Doors rock band spent the last few months of his life in Paris and died here in 1971. Fans still hold vigils at his grave, which is covered with scrawled messages from those who come from all over the world.

2. Oscar Wilde, Cimetière du Père Lachaise

The Dublin-born author died in 1900, after allegedly uttering: "My wallpaper and I are fighting a duel to the death. One or the other of us has to go." His tomb is unmissable, with a huge monument by Jacob Epstein.

3. Frédéric Chopin, Cimetière du Père Lachaise

The Polish composer was born in 1810 and died in Paris at the age of 39. The statue on his tomb represents "the genius of music sunk in grief".

4. Édith Piaf, Cimetière du Père Lachaise

The iconic French *chanteuse*, known as the "little sparrow", was born in poverty in the Belleville district of Paris in 1915, less than 1,500 m (5,000 ft) from where she was buried in 1963 in a simple black tomb.

5. Marcel Proust, Cimetière du Père Lachaise

The ultimate chronicler of the city, Proust was born in Paris in 1871. He is buried in the family tomb.

6. Samuel Beckett, Cimetière du Montparnasse

The Irish-born Nobel Prize-winning writer settled in Paris in 1937, having previously studied here. He died in 1989 and his gravestone is a simple slab, reflecting the writer's enigmatic nature.

7. Jean-Paul Sartre and Simone de Beauvoir, Cimetière du Montparnasse

Joined together in death as in life, even though they never actually lived together, their joint grave is a remarkably simple affair. Both of these philosophers were born, lived and died in Paris.

8. Sarah Bernhardt, Cimetière du Père Lachaise

A world-famous actress, Sarah Bernhardt played characters from Hamlet to Cleopatra in the late 19th and early 20th centuries, and was one of the first dramatic artists to star on screen.

9. Rosa Bonheur, Cimetière du Père Lachaise

Bonheur was a 19th-century Realist artist, whose works depicting animals are displayed in the Musée d'Orsay *(p26)*. She was a non-conformist who enjoyed traditionally male pursuits such as hunting.

10. Colette, Cimetière du Père Lachaise

One of France's most respected writers, her novel *Gigi* was adapted for the stage, when Colette famously picked a young Audrey Hepburn to play the leading role.

Places to Eat

PRICE CATEGORIES
For a three-course meal for one with half a bottle of wine (or equivalent meal), taxes and extra charges

€ under €30 €€ €30–€50 €€€ over €50

1. Le Pré Catelan
Route de Suresnes, Bois de Boulogne, 75016 Sun, Mon, Tue, 2 weeks Feb, 3 weeks Aug, 1 week Nov restaurant-leprecatelan.paris · €€€
Tucked away in the Bois de Boulogne (p160) is this high-class dining pavilion in a romantic setting with elegant service.

2. Le Baratin
3 Rue Jouye-Rouve, 75020
01 43 49 39 70 Sun & Mon · €€
A local favourite in Belleville, this bistro serves modern French cuisine with excellent wines. The fixed-price lunch is particularly popular. Vegetarian options are not available.

3. Boom Boom Villette
30 Ave Corentin Cariou 75019
boomboomvillette.com · €
Next door to Cité des Sciences et de l'Industrie (p160) is this sprawling indoor food market with 23 restaurants and bars, offering cuisines including Vietnamese, Italian and Japanese.

4. Le Camondo
D2 61 bis Rue de Monceau, 75008 lecamondo.fr · €€€
Set in the Musée Nissim de Camondo (p63), this restaurant serves modern dishes in an elegant courtyard.

5. La Closerie des Lilas
E6 171 Blvd du Montparnasse, 75006 closeriedeslilas.fr · €€
With its piano bar and terrace, this is a Montparnasse institution. The brasserie is cheaper than the main restaurant. The steak tartare is recommended.

6. Simonetta
32 Quai de la Marne, 75019
simonetta-paris.com · €€
Visitors flock to this canalside pizzeria close to the Parc de la Villette. Eat on the terrace while watching life on the water.

7. L'Assiette
181 Rue du Château, 75014
Mon & Tue restaurant-lassiette. paris · €€
This is the place to come for well-executed traditional cuisine such as cassoulet and crème caramel.

8. Gordon Ramsay au Trianon
1 Blvd de la Reine, 78000 Versailles Sun & Mon waldorfastoria versailles.fr · €€€
Gordon Ramsay's protegé Frédéric Larquemin is the chef at this Michelin-starred restaurant.

9. Le Perchoir
14 Rue Crespin du Gast, 75020
Sun D, Mon, Tue, Wed–Sat L
leperchoir.fr · €€€
Rooftop restaurant, with an open-air cocktail bar, offering innovative French dishes.

10. Brasserie Molitor
10 Ave de la Prte Molitor, 75016
molitorparis.com · €€
This brasserie offers comfort food. The favourites include toasted cheese sandwiches with truffles and burgers with smoked cheddar and onion compote.

Elegant interior of Gordon Ramsay au Trianon

STREETSMART

A shopping bag and bicycle

GETTING AROUND

Whether exploring Paris on foot or making use of public transport, here is everything you need to know to navigate the city and the areas beyond the centre like a pro.

PUBLIC TRANSPORT COSTS
Tickets are valid on all forms of public transport.

SINGLE

€2.15

(zones 1–3)

DAY TICKET

€13.95

(zones 1–3)

3-DAY TICKET

€30.90

(zones 1–3)

SPEED LIMIT

MOTORWAY

130 km/h
(80 mph)

MAJOR ROADS

80 km/h
(49 mph)

RING ROADS

70 km/h
(43 mph)

URBAN AREAS

50 km/h
(30 mph)

Arriving by Air

Paris has two major airports, Charles de Gaulle (also known as Roissy) and Orly, and one secondary airport, Beauvais, which serves mainly budget airlines. All three are well connected to the city centre by either train, bus or taxi. For information on journey times and ticket prices between Paris's airports and the city centre, see the table below.

The **Shuttle Direct** website searches the best offers for services, including shared rides, from the airports and your destination, and provides up-to-date prices for buses, taxis and other options.

The **RATP Roissybus** operates regular services from Charles de Gaulle, and RER trains (Line B) leave regularly every 5–15 minutes, calling at Gare du Nord, Châtelet-Les-Halles and several other major stations. The extension to Metro Line 14, which opened in summer 2024, connects Orly with central Paris in around 25 minutes.

The most direct way into Paris from Beauvais is by shuttle bus to Porte Maillot. Book in advance online.

RATP Roissybus
W ratp.fr/en/titres-et-tarifs/airport-tickets

Shuttle Direct
W shuttledirect.com

Train Travel

Regular high-speed trains connect Paris's six international railway stations to numerous major cities across Europe. Reservations for these services are essential, as seats get booked up quickly, particularly during peak times.

You can buy tickets and passes for multiple international journeys from **Eurail** or **Interrail**; however, you may need to pay an additional reservation fee. Always check carefully before boarding that your pass is valid on the service you wish to use.

Eurostar runs a fast, regular service from London to central Paris via the Channel Tunnel.

Students and those under 26 can benefit from discounted rail travel both to and within France. For more information, visit the Eurail or Interrail website.

Eurail
🌐 eurail.com
Eurostar
🌐 eurostar.com
Interrail
🌐 interrail.eu

Domestic Train Travel

Paris has six main stations located across the city, which all serve different regions.

The French state railway, **SNCF**, has two services in Paris: the Banlieue suburban service and the Grandes Lignes, or long-distance service. Banlieue services operate within the five-zone network. The TGV offers high-speed routes, which should be booked in advance. There are also a number of budget high-speed trains, such as **Ouigo**.

Before boarding a train, remember to time-punch *(composter)* your ticket to validate your journey; this does not apply to e-tickets. Tickets for city transport cannot be used on Banlieue trains, with the exception of some RER tickets to stations with both SNCF and RER lines.

Ouigo
🌐 ouigo.com
SNCF
🌐 sncf-connect.com

Public Transport

The metro, RER, buses and trams are all run by **RATP** (Régie Autonome des Transports Parisiens). Safety and hygiene measures, timetables, ticket information, transport maps and more can be found on their website.

RATP
🌐 ratp.fr

Tickets

The Paris metropolitan area is divided into five ticket zones. Central Paris is zone 1, Roissy-Charles-de-Gaulle Airport is in zone 5, and Orly Airport and Versailles are in zone 4. The metro network serves zones 1–3.

To avoid buying paper tickets (which are being phased out in 2025) you can buy tickets on your phone using the Bonjour RATP app or get a **Navigo** pass, a rechargeable smart card that can be used on the metro, RER and buses. The Navigo Easy costs €2 for the pass and can be topped up with credit and with as many standard fares as you like.

Visitors can also enjoy unlimited travel on the metro, RER and Paris buses with a Paris Visite pass, valid for 1, 3 or 5 consecutive days in zones 1–3, and available from the RATP.

Bus-only paper tickets can be purchased from the driver. Validate tickets using the machine on the bus.

Navigo
🌐 iledefrance-mobilites.fr

GETTING TO AND FROM THE AIRPORT

Airport	Transport	Journey Time	Price
Charles de Gaulle	RATP Roissybus	1 hr 10 mins	€16.60
	RATP 350 bus	60–80 mins	€2.15
	RATP 351 bus	70–90 mins	€2.15
	RER	25–30 mins	€11.80
	Taxi	25–45 mins	€55–62
Orly	RATP Orlybus	25–30 mins	€11.50
	Orlyval/RER	30–40 mins	€15.40
	Tram Line T7	30 mins	€2.15
	Taxi	25–45 mins	€35–41
Beauvais	Shuttle bus	1 hr 15 mins	€16.90
	Taxi	1 hr–1 hr 30 mins	from €170

Metro and RER

The Paris metro has 14 main lines and two minor lines. The RER is a system of five lines of commuter trains that travel underground in central Paris and above ground in outlying areas. The two systems overlap in the city centre. RER trips outside the city centre require special tickets; fares to suburbs and nearby towns vary.

Buses and Trams

Most buses must be flagged down at designated stops. Your ticket may be used for transfers to other bus and tramway lines for 90 minutes (between the first and last validation). Each time you change buses or trams, you must validate your ticket again. Exceptions to this rule are the Orlybus and Roissybus services, as well as lines 221, 297, 299, 350 and 351.

There are 47 night bus lines, called Noctilien, serving Paris and its suburbs. The terminus for most lines is Châtelet.

Thirteen tram lines, T1 to T13, operate in Paris, mainly servicing the outskirts of the city. You can travel on the trams using regular metro tickets and passes. They don't run past the most major tourist attractions but are a pleasant way to see the outer reaches of Paris.

Long-Distance Bus Travel

Two major coach operators, **FlixBus** and **BlaBlaCar**, link Paris to other towns in France and destinations throughout Europe. Between the two companies – low-cost alternatives to planes and trains – travellers from Paris can reach London, Brussels, Amsterdam, Milan and Barcelona, as well as Warsaw, Zagreb and Bucharest, among other cities.
BlaBlaBus
ⓦ blablacar.fr/bus
FlixBus
ⓦ flixbus.co.uk

Taxis

Taxis can be hailed in the street or from one of the 500 or so taxi ranks dotted all over the city. Fares start at around €6.60. There is usually an additional charge for more than three passengers.

Vélo taxis are motorized tricycle rickshaws that offer a green alternative to traditional taxis. **G7 Taxis** has a large fleet of electric and hybrid cars. Taxi apps such as Uber, Free Now and Bolt also operate in Paris.
G7 Taxis
ⓦ g7.fr

Driving

Driving in Paris is not recommended. Traffic is often heavy, there are many one-way streets and parking is notoriously difficult and expensive.

Driving to Paris

Autoroutes (motorways) converge on Paris from all directions. For those travelling from Britain to Paris by road, the simplest way is to use the Eurotunnel trains that run between the terminals at Folkestone and Calais, which both have direct motorway access.

Paris is surrounded by an outer ring road called the Boulevard Périphérique. All motorways leading to the capital link in to the Périphérique, which separates the city from the suburbs. Each former city gate (*porte*) corresponds to an exit onto or from the Périphérique. Arriving motorists should take time to check their destination address and consult a map of central Paris to find the closest corresponding *porte*.

To take your own car into France you must carry proof of registration, valid insurance documents, a full and valid driving licence and a passport.

Driving in Paris

Paris is a limited traffic zone and it is compulsory for all vehicles to display a Crit'Air sticker with a number ranging from 1 to 5, which denotes the level of pollution in ascending order. In the event of high pollution levels, vehicles with certain stickers may be banned from the road. The stickers can be purchased from the **Air Quality Certificate Service**.

Park in areas with a large "P" or *payant* sign on the pavement or road, and pay at the parking meter with *La Paris Carte* (available from any kiosk), a credit or debit card, or by using the PaybyPhone app *(p172)*.

Paris has numerous underground car parks, signposted by a white "P" on a blue background.

Air Quality Certificate Service
🆆 certificat-air.gouv.fr

Car Hire
To hire a car in France you must be at least 21 years old and have held a valid driver's licence for at least a year. You will also need to present a credit card to secure the rental deposit. Check the regulations regarding the type of driving licence you will need to drive in France with your local automobile association before you travel.

Ada.Paris is a self-service car hire firm that operates throughout the Paris region. You can pick up a car from one parking station, make your journey and park at any other station in the region.

Ada.Paris
🆆 ada.fr

Rules of the Road
Always drive on the right. Unless otherwise signposted, vehicles coming from the right have right of way. Cars on a roundabout usually have right of way, although the Arc de Triomphe is a hair-raising exception because cars give way to traffic on the right.

At all times, drivers must carry a valid driver's licence, registration and insurance documents. Seat belts must always be worn, and it is prohibited to sound your horn in the city. In the centre, it is against the law to use the bus lanes at all times. France strictly enforces its drink-drive limit *(p173)*.

Boats and Ferries
Several companies run regular passenger and vehicle ferry services from the UK. **P&O Ferries** offers services from Dover to Calais, **Condor Ferries** operates between Poole and St-Malo and **DFDS Seaways** runs routes from Newhaven to Dieppe and from Dover to Dunkirk and Calais. **Brittany Ferries** makes crossings from Plymouth to Roscoff, from Poole and Portsmouth to Cherbourg, and from Portsmouth to Le Havre and Caen. They also run an overnight service from Portsmouth to St-Malo.

Driving to Paris from Cherbourg takes about four hours; from Dieppe or Le Havre, about two and a half hours; and from Calais, two hours.

Brittany Ferries
🆆 brittany-ferries.co.uk
Condor Ferries
🆆 condorferries.co.uk
DFDS Seaways
🆆 dfdsseaways.co.uk
P&O Ferries
🆆 poferries.com

Paris by Boat
Paris's riverboat shuttle, the **Batobus**, runs every 20 to 45 minutes, with more frequent services in spring and summer. Tickets can be bought at Batobus stops and at RATP and tourist offices.

Batobus
🆆 batobus.com

Cycling
Paris is reasonably flat, manageably small and has many backstreets where traffic is restricted.

The **Vélib'** shared bike scheme is available 24 hours a day. There are over 1,400 Vélib' docking terminals dotted throughout the city centre and Greater Paris area; payment is made via the smartphone app or by credit card at the terminals.

Vélib'
🆆 velib-metropole.fr

Walking
Walking is by far the most agreeable way to explore central Paris. Most sights are only a short distance apart. The Office du Tourisme has walking itineraries on its website *(p175)*.

PRACTICAL INFORMATION

A little local know-how goes a long way in Paris. On these pages you can find all the essential advice and information you will need to make the most of your trip to this city.

AT A GLANCE

CURRENCY
Euro (EUR)

AVERAGE DAILY SPEND

SAVE	SPEND	SPLURGE
€65	€175	€300+

BOTTLED WATER	COFFEE	Beer	DINNER FOR TWO
€1.50	€3.50	€8	€80

ESSENTIAL PHRASES

Hello	Bonjour
Goodbye	Au revoir
Please	S'il vous plaît
Thank you	Merci
Do you speak English?	Parlez-vous anglais?
I don't understand	Je ne comprends pas

ELECTRICITY SUPPLY
Power sockets are type C and E, fitting two-pronged plugs. Standard voltage is 230 volts.

Passports and Visas

For entry requirements, including visas, consult your nearest French embassy or check the **France-Visas** website. Citizens of the UK, US, Canada, Australia and New Zealand do not need a visa for stays of up to three months, but in future must apply in advance for the European Travel Information and Authorization System (**ETIAS**); rollout has continually been postponed so check website for details. Visitors from other countries may also require an ETIAS, so check before travelling. EU nationals do not need a visa or an ETIAS.
ETIAS
W travel-europe.europa.eu/etias_en
France-Visas
W france-visas.gouv.fr

Government Advice

It is important to consult both your and the French government's advice before travelling. The UK Foreign, Commonwealth and Development Office (**FCDO**), the **US State Department**, the **Australian Department of Foreign Affairs and Trade** and **Gouvernement France** offer the latest information on security, health and local regulations.
Australian Department of Foreign Affairs and Trade
W smartraveller.gov.au
Gouvernement France
W gouvernement.fr
UK FCDO
W gov.uk/foreign-travel-advice
US State Department
W travel.state.gov

Customs Information

You can find information on the laws relating to goods and currency taken into or out of France on the official **France Customs** website. For EU citizens there are no limits on goods that can be taken into or out of France, provided they are for your personal use.
France Customs
W douane.gouv.fr

Insurance

We recommend that you take out a comprehensive policy covering theft, loss of belongings, medical care, cancellations and delays, and read the small print carefully.

EU and UK citizens are eligible for free emergency medical care in France, provided they have a valid European Health Insurance Card (EHIC) or Global Health Insurance Card (**GHIC**).

GHIC
W services.nhsbsa.nhs.uk

Vaccinations

No inoculations are needed to visit France.

Money

Most establishments accept major credit, debit and prepaid currency cards, but it's always a good idea to carry some cash too. Contactless payments are widely accepted in Paris.

Tipping in restaurants is considered polite. If you are pleased with the service a tip of 5–10% of the total bill is appreciated. Hotel porters and house-keeping generally expect a tip of €1 to €2 per bag or day. It is sufficient to tip taxi drivers €1 to €2.

Travellers with Specific Requirements

Paris's historic buildings and cobbled streets can make the city tricky to navigate. However, most of Paris's top attractions are wheelchair-accessible and there are a number of organizations working to further improve accessibility throughout France's capital.

The Office du Tourisme (p174) lists easily accessible sights, adapted public toilets and routes for visitors with mobility, visual or hearing impair-ment, while **Jaccede** has details of accessible museums, hotels, bars, restaurants and cinemas.

The **RATP** website provides detailed information on accessible public transport, including a route planner that can be tailored to your specific

needs. **SNCF**'s website has useful information on accessible train travel.

Les Compagnons du Voyage will pro-vide an escort for persons with limited mobility or visual or hearing impariment on public transport, for a fee.

Jaccede
W jaccede.com
Les Compagnons du Voyage
W compagnons.com
RATP
W ratp.fr/en/accessibilite
SNCF
W sncf-voyageurs.com

Language

French is the official language spoken in Paris. The French are fiercely proud of their language, but don't let this put you off. Mastering a few niceties goes a long way though you can get by without knowing the language at all.

Opening Hours

Most museums close either on a Monday or Tuesday, and some have a late opening one evening a week.

Some shops and businesses close for an hour or two around noon. Small shops, restaurants and bars are closed on Mondays, and most shops are closed on Sundays.

Businesses, banks, most shops and many restaurants are closed on public holidays: 1 Jan (New Year's Day), Easter Monday, 1 May (Labour Day), 8 May (VE Day), Ascension Day (40 days after Easter), Whitsun (7th Sunday after Easter), Whit Monday (the day after Whitsun), 14 July (Bastille Day), 15 August (Assumption), 1 November (All Saints' Day), 11 November (Armistice Day) and 25 December (Christmas Day).

Situations can change quickly and unexpectedly. Always check before visiting attractions and hospitality venues for up-to-date opening hours and booking requirements.

Personal Security

Paris is generally a safe city to visit. Petty theft is as common here as in most major cities. Pickpockets often frequent tourist spots, busy streets and the metro system and RER. Use your common sense, keep valuables in a safe place, and be alert to your surroundings.

AT A GLANCE

EMERGENCY NUMBERS

GENERAL EMERGENCY	FIRE SERVICE
112	**18**

POLICE	MEDICAL EMERGENCY
17	**15**

TIME ZONE

CET/CEST
Central European Summer Time (CEST) runs from end Mar to end Oct.

TAP WATER

Unless stated otherwise, tap water in France is safe to drink.

WEBSITES AND APPS

Office du Tourisme
The official Paris tourist board website (parisjetaime.com).

Le Fooding
No matter where you are in the city, find the nearest recommended restaurant in an instant.

PaybyPhone
Pay for on-street parking quickly and easily with this app.

Bonjour RATP
The official app from RATP, the city's public transport operator.

If you have anything stolen, go to the nearest police station (commissariat de police) within 24 hours, and bring ID with you. A list of police stations can be found on the Office du Tourisme website (p174). Get a copy of the crime report in order to make an insurance claim. If you have your passport stolen, contact your embassy.

When travelling late at night, avoid long transfers in metro stations such as Châtelet-Les-Halles and Montparnasse.

Paris is a diverse, multicultural city. As a rule, Parisians are accepting of all people, regardless of their race, gender or sexuality. Same-sex marriage was legalized in 2013 and France recognized the right to legally change your gender in 2016. Paris has a thriving LGBTQ+ scene, centred in the Marais district. The **Centre LGBT Paris Île-de-France** offers advice and hosts regular events.

Events in recent years have led to an increased army and police presence in Paris. Expect bag checks at most major attractions.

Centre LGBT Paris Île-de- France
🇼 centrelgbtparis.org

Health

France has a world-class healthcare system. Emergency medical care is free for all EU and UK nationals with an EHIC or GHIC (p171). You may have to pay for treatment and reclaim the money later. For visitors from outside the EU, payment of hospital and medical expenses is the patient's responsibility. It is therefore important to arrange comprehensive medical insurance before travelling.

Paris hospitals are listed on the **Assistance Publique** website. The most centrally located hospital is the Hôtel Dieu (Pl du Parvis Notre-Dame).

Seek medicinal supplies and advice for minor ailments from pharmacies identifiable by a green cross. Each pharmacy will display details of the nearest 24-hour service on the door.

Assistance Publique
🇼 aphp.fr

Smoking, Alcohol and Drugs

Smoking is prohibited in all public places, but is allowed on restaurant, café and pub outside terraces, as long as they are not enclosed.

The possession of narcotics is prohibited and may result in a prison sentence.

Unless stated otherwise, alcohol consumption on the streets is permitted. France has a strict limit of 0.05 per cent BAC (blood alcohol content) for drivers.

ID

There is no requirement for visitors to carry ID, but in the event of a routine check you may be asked to show your passport. If you don't have it with you, the police may escort you to wherever your passport is being kept.

Local Customs

Etiquette (la politesse) is important to Parisians. On entering a store or café, you are expected to say *"bonjour"* to staff, and when leaving, *"au revoir"*. Be sure to add *"s'il vous plaît"* (please) when ordering something and *"pardon"* if you bump into someone accidentally.

The French usually shake hands on meeting someone for the first time. Those who know each other well greet each other with a kiss on each cheek. If you are unsure what's expected, wait to see if they proffer a hand or a cheek.

Responsible Travel

There are plenty of ways to travel responsibly while in Paris, including by embracing locally and sustainably sourced cuisine and using reusable bags and water bottles. For the latter, there are countless water fountains across the city where you can fill up – find a map at **Eau de Paris**. You can also reduce your carbon footprint by walking or cycling around the city. Paris now has around 1,000 km (620 miles) of cycle lanes, making exploring by bike easier and safer than ever. This is set to increase hugely over the next few years, with the aim of making the whole city cycle-friendly by 2026.

Eau de Paris
w eaudeparis.fr/en

Mobile Phones and Wi-Fi

Free Wi-Fi hotspots dotted all over Paris provide fast internet access in more than 260 public places, including museums, parks and libraries. These are clearly signposted with the Paris Wi-Fi logo. Cafés and restaurants offer free Wi-Fi for those making a purchase.

Visitors with EU tariffs will be able to use their devices abroad without being affected by data roaming charges. Users will be charged the same rates for data, SMS and voice calls as they would pay at home. Those not on EU tariffs should check roaming rates with their provider.

Post

Stamps (timbres) can be bought at post offices and tabacs (tobacconists). Most post offices have self-service machines to weigh and frank your mail.

Taxes and Refunds

VAT is around 20 percent in France. Non-EU residents can claim back tax on certain goods. Look out for the Global Refund Tax-Free sign, where the retailer will supply a form and issue a détaxe receipt. Present the goods receipt, détaxe receipt and your passport at customs when you depart to receive your refund.

Discount Cards

Entry to some national and municipal museums is free on the first Sunday of each month.

Visitors under 18 years of age and EU passport holders aged 18–26 years are usually admitted free of charge to national museums. There are sometimes discounts for students and those over 60 who have ID showing their date of birth.

The **Paris Pass** offers access to more than 90 attractions for 2, 3, 4 or 6 consecutive days. It also includes a ticket for a hop-on hop-off bus tour.

Paris Pass
w parispass.com

PLACES TO STAY

Paris is overflowing with places to stay, from grand mansions to cute boutique hotels. The best area to stay in depends on what you want: for example, Île de la Cité has offerings conveniently located next to some of the city's most iconic sights, while Montmartre is for those seeking a more bohemian feel.

Paris's nightly city tax is not quoted with the room rate, and can vary from €2.60 per person for hostels to €14.95 per person for the most luxurious of the city's hotels.

PRICE CATEGORIES

For a standard, double room per night (with breakfast if included), taxes and extra charges.

€ under $150
€€ $150–$350
€€€ over $350

Île de la Cité and Île St-Louis

Hôtel Des Deux-Îles

📍P4 🏠59 Rue Saint-Louis en l'Île 75004 🌐deuxiles-paris-hotel.com · €€

Just minutes on foot from Notre-Dame, the location of this cosy hotel takes some beating. But that's not all it has going for it: the service is warm and the breakfasts delicious, made using fresh produce from local businesses. And while, yes, the rooms are small, they're also beautifully decorated.

Hôtel Du Jeu De Paume

📍P4 🏠54 Rue Saint-Louis en l'Île 75004 🌐jeude paumehotel.com · €€

Standing on the site of a 17th-century tennis court owned by Louis XIII, this historic, family-run hotel offers an old-world feel thanks to its exposed wooden beams and rustic stone walls. Don't miss the pretty plant-filled courtyard garden or the sauna and fitness area located in the vaulted cellars.

Beaubourg and Les Halles

Hôtel Crayon Rouge

📍M1 🏠42 Rue Croix des Petits Champs, 75001 🌐hotelcrayonrouge.com · €€

Colourful wallpaper and retro furniture are the name of the game at this charmingly kooky hotel. The self-service wine bar (courtesy of the wine-loving owners) is a nice touch and the location, a stone's throw from the Louvre, is excellent.

Hôtel du Sentier

📍F3 🏠48 Rue du Caire, 75002 🌐hoteldusentier.com · €€

If you've ever dreamt of living in a Parisian pied-à-terre, then the Hôtel du Sentier is a must. The chic rooms here have gorgeous views over the city from Juliet balconies.

Hôtel Madame Rêve

📍M1 🏠48 Rue du Louvre, 75001 🌐madamereve.com · €€€

Beautiful rooms decked out with polished wood furnishings and a two-star Michelin restaurant are undoubted draws of this opulent hotel. But the biggest selling point? A vast rooftop terrace offering incredible views over Notre-Dame.

Marais and the Bastille

Hôtel Caron de Beaumarchais

📍Q3 🏠12 Rue Vieille du Temple, 75004 🌐caron debeaumarchais.com · €

A seven-storey sliver of a hotel, this spot looks like an old-world dolls' house from the outside – and the inside is no different. Here, the walls are covered in floral wallpaper and vintage paintings, while the chandeliers illuminate brocade chairs, classical musical instruments and a card table.

Hôtel du Petit Moulin Paris

📍R2 🏠29 Rue de Poitou, 75003 🌐hotelpetitmoulin paris.com · €€

Housed in an historic boulangerie dating from the time of Henri IV, this boutique hotel is packed full of character. The rooms are joyfully eclectic: think velvet blankets, space-age, 1960s-style furniture and lavish patterned wallpaper.

Hôtel National Des Arts et Métiers

📍 G3 🏠 243 Rue Saint-Martin, 75003 🌐 hotel national.paris · €€€

Minimalist, understated and impossibly chic, this hotel feels like the house of a well-to-do architect. The exquisitely designed rooms are painted in muted, calming colours, dotted with contemporary furniture, and adjoin stylish bathrooms.

Le Pavillon de la Reine

📍 R3 🏠 28 Pl des Vosges, 75003 🌐 pavillon-de-la-reine.com · €€€

Plant-lovers, this one's for you; creeping plants cover virtually every inch of the façade of this grande dame, found right on Place des Vosges. The leafy courtyard feels like a true respite from the city, and the bedrooms are reminiscent of an English stately home.

Tuileries and Opéra Quarters

Chouchou

📍 E2 🏠 23 Bd de Sébastopol, 75001 🌐 chouchouhotel.com · €€

While the rooms here are on the small side, they're beautiful, with parquet flooring and stylish velvet

armchairs, plus nice little touches like pretty dried flowers. Another popular, if unusual, added extra are the private bath tubs for hire in the basement.

Hôtel Petit Lafayette

📍 F2 🏠 46 Rue de Trévise, 75009 🌐 hotel-lafayette-paris.com · €€

This diminutive boutique hotel is the perfect spot for families visiting Paris. Parents can loan prams for little ones, while older kids can use the hotel's scooters. It's also a great shout for shoppers, being right on the doorstep of the Grands Magasins.

La Fantaisie

📍 F2 🏠 24 Rue Cadet, 75009 🌐 lafantaisie.com · €€€

Head inside this hotel and you'll feel like you've stepped straight into *Alice in Wonderland*. The ceilings of the communal spaces are decorated with brightly painted flowers, while on the walls are colourful artworks. And there's even a charming, flower-filled courtyard garden – perfect for a Madhatter-style tea party.

Ritz Paris

📍 E3 🏠 15 Pl Vendôme, 75001 🌐 ritzparis.com · €€€

Feel like royalty at this legendary hotel, whose luxurious rooms wouldn't look out of place inside Versailles. There's everything you could ever ask for, including a shopping

arcade, a spa and multiple bars and restaurants. The service is so good it's almost theatrical.

Champs-Élysées

Pley

📍 C2 🏠 214 Rue du Faubourg Saint-Honoré, 75008 🌐 pley-hotel.com · €

Radio-themed to hark back to its previous life as a broadcasting space, the hotel is chock-full of musical paraphernalia. Rooms are spacious and stylish (particularly considering the price point) and the large bar-restaurant is a delight.

citizenM Paris Champs Élysées

📍 C3 🏠 128 Rue La Boétie, 75008 🌐 citizenm.com · €€

Built for efficiency rather than charm, all of the rooms at citizenM are identical. Yet what they lack in character they make up for in comfort: think huge beds, widescreen TVs and excellent shower pressure.

Le Bristol

📍 D3 🏠 112 Rue du Faubourg Saint-Honoré 🌐 oethercollection.com · €€€

With its top-notch service, impeccably decorated rooms and three-starred Michelin restaurant, this palatial spot can hold its own against Paris's most upmarket hotels. The huge courtyard garden is another plus.

Eiffel Tower and Invalides

Hôtel du Champ de Mars

🏠 7 Rue du Champ de Mars, 75007 🌐 hoteldu champdemars.com · €

It might be tucked away down a quiet residential street, but this family-run hotel is still close to the action, with the Hôtel des Invalides and Eiffel Tower a short stroll away. Expect chic little rooms, complete with floral wallpaper, soft furnishings and fresh flowers.

J.K. Place Paris

📍 D4 🏠 82 Rue de Lille, 75007 🌐 jkplace.paris · €€€

Visiting this intimate hotel feels a little like being in a gallery, with artworks and antiques decorating almost every corner. There's more than art to delight here, though, with a stunning spa, upscale restaurant and impeccable service.

Shangri-La Paris

📍 B3 🏠 10 Ave d'Iéna, 75116 🌐 shangri-la.com · €€€

Once the private home of French prince Roland Bonaparte, a celebrated geographer and botanist, this hotel is opulence writ large, with rooms decked out with rich tapestries, gold gilding and plush fabrics. An unexpected bonus? Le Bar Botaniste, where the cocktails are inspired by Roland's botanical trips through Europe and Asia.

St-Germain, Latin and Luxembourg Quarters

Solar Hotel

📍 D6 🏠 22 Rue Boulard, 75014 🌐 solarhotel.fr · €

The no-frills rooms at this hotel are rather plain, but they do the trick – and for a great price. Plus, Solar's commitment to being eco-responsible is strong: breakfast is organic, much of the decor is made from recycled materials and there's free bicycle hire.

Hôtel Dame des Arts

📍 M4 🏠 4 Rue Danton, 75006 🌐 damedesarts. com · €€

This hotel is a multi-sensory experience. There are the whiffs of the hotel's signature scent as you stroll the corridors; spellbinding views from its terrace, including over Notre-Dame and Saint-Sulpice; and the smooth feel of handcrafted wooden equipment in the gym.

Jardin des Plantes

Hotel le Lapin Blanc

📍 M5 🏠 41 Bd Saint-Michel, 75005 🌐 hotel-lapin-blanc.com · €

Housed in one of Paris's oldest neighbourhoods, the "white rabbit" offers a contemporary contrast to its historic surroundings. The hotel has a bright, modern and somewhat whimsical feel, with rooms decorated in an Easter-esque palette of pastel shades.

Hôtel des Grandes Écoles

📍 N6 🏠 75 Rue du Cardinal Lemoine, 75005 🌐 hotel desgrandesecoles.com · €

Painted shutters, trailing ivy and leafy surrounds: this hotel feels like it belongs in Provence, rather than Paris. The rooms can feel a bit old-fashioned, with oodles of flowery wallpaper and lace tablecloths, but they're comfortable, cosy and extremely reasonable in terms of price.

Hôtel Jardin de Cluny

📍 N5 🏠 9 Rue du Sommerard, 75005 🌐 hoteljardindecluny.com · €€

This cute hotel in Paris's Latin Quarter is green: both literally and figuratively. Countless leafy plants cluster here and there, and the rooms are decked in botanical William Morris-style wallpaper. The hotel has also been awarded the Ecolabel for environmentally friendly hotels, thanks to its commitment to low energy consumption and, where possible, use of renewables.

Montmartre and Pigalle

Amour Hotel

📍 F2 🏠 8 Rue de Navarin, 75009 🌐 hotelamour paris.fr · €

Risqué, punk-style vibes are the order of the day at Amour Hotel. Expect things like skull-shaped lamps, saucy artwork and disco balls. The only thing to break the trend is the plant-filled, glass-roofed courtyard restaurant, which is a pretty place to grab a bite to eat.

Le Pigalle

E1 **9 Rue Frochot, 75009** **lepigalle.paris · €€**

Staying in this hotel feels like visiting the home of your coolest friend. Downstairs are comfy leather sofas, a vinyl record library and packed bookshelves, while the rooms themselves are decorated with an eclectic mix of posters and street photography. The on-site events, including DJ nights, are a bonus.

Maison Mère

F2 **7 Rue Mayran, 75009** **maisonmere.co · €€**

One for the business travellers and digital nomads, Maison Mère has an on-site coworking space and a big emphasis on super-fast Wi-Fi. The smallest rooms are really quite miniscule, but the large communal spaces make up for it, as does the sociable cocktail bar (which offers live jazz concerts every Thursday). It's also ideal for those with specific accessibility requirements.

Maison Souquet

E1 **10 Rue de Bruxelles, 75009** **maisonsouquet. com · €€€**

A pleasure house during the early 1900s, this lavish hotel, nestled in bohemian Montmartre, harks back to the time of the belle époque. A mixture of tasselled lamps, plum-coloured velvet armchairs and Moorish-inspired woodwork give the interior a rich, sumptuous feel, as do the oil paintings in gilded frames that line the walls. Don't miss the gilded spa and pool.

Greater Paris

Hôtel Les Deux Gares

G2 **2 Rue des Deux Gares, 75010** **hoteldeux gares.com · €**

Nestled between Gare du Nord and Gare de l'Est, this hotel is a handy choice for travellers on the hop. But that's not the only reason to visit. The joyful, vibrant rooms here – which look like they were designed by Wes Anderson himself – are utterly eye-catching, while the charming little café-restaurant is very good value.

Mama Shelter Paris West

20 Ave de la Prte de la Plaine, 75015 **mama shelter.com · €**

This kitschy hotel might be a metro ride away from the city centre, but it makes up for that with a buzzing social scene, making this a great choice for solo travellers looking to mix and mingle. Expect plenty of live music, an expansive roof terrace and a well-stocked bar.

Babel

6 Rue Gambetta, 93400 Saint-Ouen-sur-Seine **babel-belleville.com · €**

An affordable hotel in up-and-coming Belleville, Babel boasts welcoming – if small – rooms, with comfortable beds, sound-proof walls and refillable natural toiletries. Bahar, its Silk Road-French fusion restaurant, is a big hit with locals; here, spice-laden dishes are washed down with local beers and natural wines.

Mob Hotel

3 Rue Lemon, 75020 **mobhotel.com · €**

Travelling solo? Make for Mob. This hotel is the perfect place to meet like-minded new friends, thanks to its expansive communal spaces. Play ping pong, catch a live music performance or watch a film on the huge outdoor screen in the courtyard. The bar and restaurant are also great places to bond.

Hôtel Molitor

A2 **13 Rue Nungesser et Coli, 75016** **molitor paris.com · €€**

Rooms at this hotel are clean and comfortable, but the star of the show has to be its huge 46-m (151-ft) pool. It's no wonder, really, as the cruise ship-style building started off life as a popular outdoor pool in the 1920s, when Parisians would come to swim sunbathe – it's still a great spot for some leisurely lounging today.

INDEX

PHRASE BOOK

In an Emergency

Help!	Au secours!	oh sekoor
Stop!	Arrêtez!	aret-ay
Call…	Appelez…	apuh-lay
…a doctor!	…un médecin!	uñ medsañ
…an ambulance!	…une ambulance!	oon oñboo-loñs
…the police!	…la police!	lah poh-lees
…the fire brigade!	…les pompiers!	leh poñ-peeyay

Communication Essentials

Yes/No	Oui/Non	wee/noñ
Please	S'il vous plaît	seel voo play
Thank you	Merci	mer-see
Excuse me	Excusez-moi	exkoo-zay mwah
Hello	Bonjour	boñzhoor
Goodbye	Au revoir	oh ruh-vwar
Good evening	Bonsoir	boñ-swar
What?	Quel, quelle?	kel, kel
When?	Quand?	koñ
Why?	Pourquoi?	poor-kwah
Where?	Où?	oo

Useful Phrases

How are you?	Comment allez-vous?	kom-moñ talay voo
Very well,	Très bien,	treh byañ
Pleased to meet you.	Enchanté de faire votre connaissance.	oñshoñ-tay duh fehr votr koñ-ay-sans
Where is/are…?	Où est/sont…?	oo ay/soñ
Which way to..?	Quelle est la direction pour..?	kel ay lah deer-ek-syoñ poor
Do you speak English?	Parlez-vous anglais?	par-lay voo oñg-lay
I don't understand.	Je ne comprends pas.	zhuh nuh kom-proñ pah
I'm sorry.	Excusez-moi.	exkoo-zay mwah

Useful Words

big	grand	groñ
small	petit	puh-tee
hot	chaud	show
cold	froid	frwah
good	bon	boñ
bad	mauvais	moh-veh
open	ouvert	oo-ver
closed	fermé	fer-meh
left	gauche	gohsh
right	droit	drwah
entrance	l'entrée	l'on-tray
exit	la sortie	lah sor-tee
toilet	les toilettes	leh twah-let

Shopping

How much is it?	Ça fait combien?	sa fay kom-byañ
What time…	A quelle heure…	ah kel urr
…do you open?	…êtes-vous ouvert?	et-voo oo-ver
…do you close?	…êtes-vous fermé?	et-voo fer-may
Do you have?	Est-ce que vous avez?	es-kuh voo zavay

I would like …	Je voudrais…	zhuh voo-dray
Do you take credit cards?	Est-ce que vous acceptez les cartes de crédit?	es-kuh voo zaksept-ay leh kart duh krehdee
This one.	Celui-ci.	suhl-wee-see
That one.	Celui-là.	suhl-wee-lah
expensive	cher	shehr
cheap	pas cher, bon marché,	pah shehr, boñ mar-shay
size, clothes	la taille	lah tye
size, shoes	la pointure	lah pwañ-tur

Types of Shop

antique shop	le magasin d'antiquités	luh maga-zañ d'oñteekee-tay
bakery	la boulangerie	lah booloñ-zhuree
bank	la banque	lah boñk
bookshop	la librairie	lah lee-brehree
cake shop	la pâtisserie	lah patee-sree
cheese shop	la fromagerie	lah fromazh-ree
chemist	la pharmacie	lah farmah-see
department store	le grand magasin	luh groñ maga-zañ
delicatessen	la charcuterie	lah sharkoot-ree
gift shop	le magasin de cadeaux	luh maga-zañ duh kadoh
greengrocer	le marchand de légumes	luh mar-shoñ duh lay-goom
grocery	l'alimentation	alee-moñtasyoñ
market	le marché	luh marsh-ay
newsagent	le magasin de journaux	luh maga-zañ duh zhoor-no
post office	la poste, le bureau de poste, le PTT	lah pohst, booroh luh duh pohst, luh peh-teh-teh
supermarket	le supermarché	luh soo pehr-marshay
tobacconist	le tabac	luh tabah
travel agent	l'agence de voyages	l'azhoñs duh vwayazh

Sightseeing

art gallery	la galerie d'art	lah galer-ree dart
bus station	la gare routière	lah gahr roo-tee-yehr
cathedral	la cathédrale	lah katay-dral
church	l'église	l'aygleez
garden	le jardin	luh zhar-dañ
library	la bibliothèque	lah beebleeo-tek
museum	le musée	luh moo-zay
railway station	la gare (SNCF)	lah gahr (es-en-say-ef)
tourist office	l'office du tourisme	ohfees doo tooreesm
town hall	l'hôtel de ville	l'ohtel duh veel

Staying in a Hotel

Do you have a vacant room?	Est-ce que vous avez une chambre?	es-kuh voo-zavay oon shambr
I have a reservation.	J'ai fait une réservation.	zhay fay oon rayzehrva-syoñ
single room	la chambre à une personne	lah shambr ah oon pehr-son
twin room	la chambre à deux lits	lah shambr ah duh lee

| room with a bath, shower | la chambre avec salle de bains, une douche | *lah shambr avek sal duh bañ, oon doosh* |
| double room, with a double bed | la chambre à deux personnes, avec un grand lit | *lah shambr ah duh pehr-son avek un gronñ lee* |

Eating Out

Have you got a table?	Avez-vous une table libre?	*avay-voo oon tahbl duh leebr*
I want to reserve a table.	Je voudrais réserver une table.	*zhuh voo-dray rayzehr-vay oon tahbl*
The bill, please.	L'addition, s'il vous plaît.	*l'adee-syoñ seel voo play*
waitress/ waiter	Madame, Mademoiselle/ Monsieur	*mah-dam, mah-demwahzel/ muh-syuh*
menu	le menu, la carte	*luh men-oo, lah kart*
fixed-price menu	le menu à prix fixe	*luh men-oo ah pree feeks*
cover charge	le couvert	*luh koo-vehr*
wine list	la carte des vins	*lah kart-deh vañ*
glass	le verre	*luh vehr*
bottle	la bouteille	*lah boo-tay*
knife	le couteau	*luh koo-toh*
fork	la fourchette	*lah for-shet*
spoon	la cuillère	*lah kwee-yehr*
breakfast	le petit déjeuner	*luh puh-tee deh-zhuh-nay*
lunch	le déjeuner	*luh deh-zhuh-nay*
dinner	le dîner	*luh dee-nay*
main course	le plat principal	*luh plah prañsee-pal*
starter, first course	l'entrée, le hors d'oeuvre	*l'oñ-tray, luh or-duhvr*
dish of the day	le plat du jour	*luh plah doo zhoor*
wine bar	le bar à vin	*luh bar ah vañ*
café	le café	*luh ka-fay*

Menu Decoder

baked	cuit au four	*kweet oh foor*
beef	le boeuf	*luh buhf*
beer	la bière	*lah bee-yehr*
boiled	bouilli	*boo-yee*
bread	le pain	*luh pan*
butter	le beurre	*luh burr*
cake	le gâteau	*luh gah-toh*
cheese	le fromage	*luh from-azh*
chicken	le poulet	*luh poo-lay*
chips	les frites	*leh freet*
chocolate	le chocolat	*luh shoko-lah*
coffee	le café	*luh kah-fay*
dessert	le dessert	*luh deh-ser*
duck	le canard	*luh kanar*
egg	l'oeuf	*l'uf*
fish	le poisson	*luh pwah-ssoñ*
fresh fruit	le fruit frais	*luh frwee freh*
garlic	l'ail	*l'eye*
grilled	grillé	*gree-yay*
ham	le jambon	*luh zhoñ-boñ*
ice, ice cream	la glace	*lah glas*
lamb	l'agneau	*l'anyoh*
lemon	le citron	*luh see-troñ*
lemon juice	le citron pressé	*luh see-troñ presseh*
meat	la viande	*lah vee-yand*
milk	le lait	*luh leh*

mineral water	l'eau minérale	*l'oh meeney-ral*
oil	l'huile	*l'weel*
onions	les oignons	*leh zonyoñ*
orange juice	l'orange pressée	*l'oroñzh presseh*
pepper	le poivre	*luh pwavr*
pork	le porc	*luh por*
potatoes	les pommes de terre	*leh pom duh tehr*
rice	le riz	*luh ree*
roast	rôti	*row-tee*
salt	le sel	*luh sel*
sausage	la saucisse	*lah sohsees*
seafood	les fruits de mer	*leh frwee duh mer*
snails	les escargots	*leh zes-kar-goh*
soup	la soupe, le potage	*lah soop, luh poh-tazh*
steak	le bifteck, le steak	*luh beef-tek, luh stek*
sugar	le sucre	*luh sookr*
tea	le thé	*luh tay*
vegetables	les légumes	*leh lay-goom*
vinegar	le vinaigre	*luh veenaygr*
water	l'eau	*l'oh*
red wine	le vin rouge	*luh vañ roozh*
white wine	le vin blanc	*luh vañ bloñ*

Numbers

0	zéro	*zeh-roh*
1	un, une	*uñ, oon*
2	deux	*duh*
3	trois	*trwah*
4	quatre	*katr*
5	cinq	*sañk*
6	six	*sees*
7	sept	*set*
8	huit	*weet*
9	neuf	*nerf*
10	dix	*dees*
11	onze	*oñz*
12	douze	*dooz*
13	treize	*trehz*
14	quatorze	*katorz*
15	quinze	*kañz*
16	seize	*sehz*
17	dix-sept	*dees-set*
18	dix-huit	*dees-weet*
19	dix-neuf	*dees-nerf*
20	vingt	*vañ*
30	trente	*tront*
40	quarante	*karoñt*
50	cinquante	*sañkoñt*
60	soixante	*swasoñt*
70	soixante-dix	*swasoñt-dees*
80	quatre-vingts	*katr-vañ*
90	quatre-vingt-dix	*katr-vañ-dees*
100	cent	*soñ*
1,000	mille	*meel*

Time

one minute	une minute	*oon mee-noot*
one hour	une heure	*oon urr*
half an hour	une demi-heure	*urr duh-me urr*
one day	un jour	*urr zhorr*
Monday	lundi	*luñ-dee*
Tuesday	mardi	*mar-dee*
Wednesday	mercredi	*mehrkruh-dee*
Thursday	jeudi	*zhuh-dee*
Friday	vendredi	*voñdruh-dee*
Saturday	samedi	*sam-dee*
Sunday	dimanche	*dee-moñsh*

ACKNOWLEDGMENTS

This edition updated by

Contributors Eleanor Aldridge, Anna Richards, Vivian Song

Senior Editor Alison McGill

Senior Designers Laura O'Brien, Vinita Venugopal

Project Editors Rachel Laidler, Tijana Todorinović

Editor Anjasi N.N., Anuroop Sanwalia

Designer Sulagna Das

Proofreader Ben Ffrancon Dowds

Indexer Vanessa Bird

Picture Researcher Manager Taiyaba Khatoon

Senior Picture Researcher Nishwan Rasool

Assistant Picture Research Administrator Manpreet Kaur

Publishing Assistant Simona Velikova

Jacket Designer Laura O'Brien

Jacket Picture Researcher Adrienne Pitts

Senior Cartographer James MacDonald

Cartography Manager Suresh Kumar

Project Cartographer Ashif

Cartography Simonetta Giori

Senior DTP Designer Tanveer Zaidi

DTP Designer Rohit Rojal, Raman Panwar

Pre-production Manager Balwant Singh

Image Retouching-Production Manager Pankaj Sharma

Production Controller Kariss Ainsworth

Managing Editors Shikha Kulkarni, Beverly Smart, Hollie Teague

Managing Art Editor Gemma Doyle

Senior Managing Art Editor Priyanka Thakur

Art Director Maxine Pedliham

Publishing Director Georgina Dee

DK would like to thank the following for their contribution to the previous editions: Patricia Baker, Kate Berens, Donna Dailey, Mike Gerrard, Bryan Pirolli, Ruth Reisenberger, M Astella Saw.

The publisher would like to thank the following for their kind permission to reproduce their photographs:

Buvette: Nicole Franzen 157.

Clair de Reve: 84.

Dorling Kindersley: CNHMS, Paris / Neil Lukas 42bl, Sacre-Coeur / Max Alexander 36bl.

Dreamstime.com: Andersastphoto 109t, Andreykr 15bc, Anyaberkut 13cl, Aprescindere 91tr, Bargotiphotography 15clb, Yulia Belousova 77tr, Bennymarty 21br, Marco Brivio 159t, Chbm89 151br, Svetlana Day 47tr, Demerzel21 35bl, 65br, 127br, Matthew Dixon 58t, Viorel Dudau 16tc, 110br, Ekaterinabelova 16cla, Evolove 121t, Flynt 117br, Ruslan Gilmanshin 45br, Guillohmz 17tr, Jlabouyrie 139tr, Sergii Kolesnyk 110bl, 113t, Maryna Kordiumova 12cra, Mistervlad 60b, 74t, Michael Mulkens 61tl, Neirfy 82b, Olrat 160bl, Massimo Parisi 116bl, Muscat Patrice 62br, Mykhailo Pavlov 46-47b, William Perry 15crb, 21c, 45cb, Kovalenkov Petr 138bl, 147br, Janusz Piekowski 74br, Rusel1981 141tl, Sborisov 12crb, Jozef Sedmak 52br, Serge001 114tl, Darius Strazdas 16tr, UlyssePixel 105tr, Pavlo Vakhrushev 13cl (8), Vitalyedush 15tr, Dennis Van De Water 54tl, 148-149, Zatletic 45bl.

Epicure: 119.

Getty Images: 500px / Vibgyor78 35cb, Corbis Historical / Hulton Deutsch 9br, Image Source / Ben Pipe Photography 49, Keystone-France / Gamma-Keystone 32tr, Moment / Alexander Spatari 13clb, 19, 34t, 39t, Moment / Artur Debat 133t, Moment / Jinna van Ringen Photography 5, Stockbyte / Paul Simcock 35br, Stone / Jeremy Walker 79, Stone / Julian Elliott Photography 31bl, Stone / P Deliss 31crb, The Image Bank / John Elk III 30t.

Getty Images / iStock: Asab974 75tr, Conejota 11br, E+ / Consu1961 31br, E+ / Pawel Gaul 20br, E+ / Pawel.Gaul 13bl, GlobalP 14bl, LembiBuchanan 73t, Neyya 68br, Omersukrugoksu 21tc, StockByM 16br, The Image Bank / Jupiterimages 167.

Gordon Ramsay au Trianon: 165.

Maison Le Roux: 137.

Marian Goodman Gallery: Rebecca Fanuele 99.

Monsieur Bleu: Adrien Dirand 125.

Musee Gustave Moreau: RMN-Grand Palais / Franck Raux 155.

Pitanga: 92.

Restaurant Chez Paul: Jessica Hauf 103.

Shakespeare and Company: Tobias Staebler 136.

Shutterstock.com: ColorMaker 70tr, Frederic Legrand - Comeo 76b, D.serra1 46cra, KievVictor 128b, Franck Legros 53br, Puripat Lertpunyaroj 43b, Andy Soloman 164tl, Theerawan 69br.

SuperStock: 4x5 Coll-Peter Willi 24tr.

Unsplash: Alex Harmuth 6-7.

Sheet Map Cover Image:
4Corners: Susanne Kremer.

Cover images:
Front and Spine: **4Corners:** Susanne Kremer. Back: **Getty Images:** Image Source / Ben Pipe Photography tl; **Getty Images / iStock:** GlobalP cl; **Unsplash:** Alex Harmuth tr.

All other images © Dorling Kindersley Limited

For further information see: www.dkimages.com

Illustrator:
Chris Orr & Associates

First edition 2002

Published in Great Britain by
Dorling Kindersley Limited,
DK, One Embassy Gardens, 8 Viaduct
Gardens, London SW11 7BW, UK

The authorised representative in the EEA is
Dorling Kindersley Verlag GmbH. Arnulfstr.
124, 80636 Munich, Germany

Published in the United States by
DK Publishing, 1745 Broadway, 20th Floor,
New York, NY 10019, USA

The publishers cannot accept responsibility for any consequences
arising from the use of this book, nor for any material on third party
websites, and cannot guarantee that any website address in this
book will be a suitable source of travel information.

A CIP catalog record is available
from the British Library.

A catalog record for this book is available
from the Library of Congress.

ISSN: 1479-344X

ISBN: 978-0-2416-7658-5

Printed and bound in China

www.dk.com

This book was made with Forest
Stewardship Council™ certified
paper – one small step in DK's
commitment to a sustainable future.
Learn more at **www.dk.com/uk/
information/sustainability**